How I Came Out and Stayed Out

How I Came Out *and* Stayed Out

Astacia Jones

Copyright @2019 by Astacia Jones,
How I Came Out *and* Stayed Out

All rights reserved.

ISBN: 978-1072-6-7384-2

Unless otherwise stated, all scripture quotations are taken from
New King James Version(NKJV) of the Bible.

No reproduction, copy or transmission of this publication may be made without written permission. No part of this publication may be reproduced, copied (photocopying), or transmitted, electronically or save in any storage mean with written permission of the author in accordance with the provisions of the International Copyright Law. Except for brief quotations in critical reviews or articles, any person who does any unauthorized act in relation to this publication may be liable to criminal prosecution and civil claims for damages.

Published by BKC Consulting, www.BKC.name/consulting
Tel: +233244961121, info@BKC.name

Contents

PART III

Introduction

I MET ASTACIA A LITTLE OVER A DECADE AGO, when we were both in college. She was fun to be around and passionate about God. We spent lots of time together, sometimes laughing and fellowshipping and sometimes guzzling down caffeine right before an all-night prayer. But mainly, we were seeking God with all of our hearts.

Over the years, I've been inspired by the woman she's become. I've seen her speak truth to young men and women about real-life issues like depression, sex, and suicide. I've seen young ladies crowd her school counseling office and cling to her, just wanting to be in her presence. And no wonder, because she's been a safe place for so many of them.

Perhaps the thing I respect the most about her is that she's a self-feeder. She knows how to initiate growth in her life, how to access help, and how to get to the places she envisions in her mind. As you read through her transformation in this book, you'll see that these qualities have been instrumental in her journey out of homosexuality.

Working with her story has reminded me, once again, that it's not about how we start-it's how we finish. We're not usually in control of things that happened to us at a young age, but we can certainly, with God in us, overcome the challenges these things have brought into our lives.

May you enjoy reading this story as much as I've enjoyed editing it. And may you, too, be encouraged to overcome, no matter what that looks like for you.

"And to he who overcomes, I will give the crown of life"
- Revelation 2:7

....

Kelani Daniels,
Editor

Part I

Chapter 1

I WAS ONLY FIVE YEARS OLD THE FIRST TIME IT HAPPENED. Single motherhood was no joke, and my mom couldn't always be home. With my dad not regularly in the picture, she lived the single mom reality: hustle hard to provide, then try to be present.

The only upside was that we lived with my grandma, so my mom didn't have to worry about who was gonna watch me when she couldn't. In her eyes, living in a relative's home was just a stepping stone on the road to us having our own place.

I would often spend days alone in my room, playing and thinking and reading. I was an only child at the time, with no other children my age in the family. Another relative lived in the house also, an uncle, and for the most part he kept to himself. Except for one day, when he invited me to his room.

"Hey Stacey, I have something to show you," he said. He

usually kept to himself as well, so I was excited that he wanted to show me something that belonged to him, and I followed him eagerly.

He shut the door behind me and I looked around the room in expectation.

When I turned back around, his pants were down.

I was so caught by surprise, I think my body instinctively froze. Since I couldn't move, I couldn't cover my eyes when he began touching himself and saying how fun it was. "Now you try," he said.

I didn't know what to do, and my little heart was telling me this was a no-no. But fear has a way of forcing obedience, so I did as he demonstrated. He continued on. When he was satisfied, he pulled up his pants and exited the room. Embarrassed and scared, I hastily put my clothes back on and went to my mine.

In the following weeks and months, the dynamic between he and myself began to change. It was as if, in his eyes, the first encounter in his room gave permission for more like it. He would catch me in the bathroom, living room, and basically any other room in the home, reveal himself, and pressure me to masturbate and perform other sexual activities with him.

At first, I was obviously very uncomfortable and scared. After all, what other kids my age were doing this kind of thing? And what if my classmates were to find out? As time passed, however, I became less scared. Weeks turned into months, and at five years old, I was more comfortable than any kindergartener should be with sexual activity.

On one of these now regular occasions, we were in a room and my uncle had me lay back on his lap. He began his usual caressing when all of a sudden, my grandmother walked in.

She froze. "David, what are you doing?"

My heart pounded wildly. He said nothing.

I laid there, not knowing what else to do. After what felt like hours, my grandmother silently walked out of the room, closing the door on my heart's ability to trust in the protection of adults.

I didn't feel safe to share any of these experiences with either of my parents because I wasn't confident they would listen or help me. So I kept to myself. In my little mind, I'd already decided the world wasn't fair and people you love couldn't be trusted. Not knowing what else to do, I housed all the confusion and fear in my soul, choosing to confide in no one.

A couple years later, when my mom was financially stable, we moved out of my grandmother's house and into a duplex. I was relieved that it was just me, my little sister, and my mom. Without my uncle's dark and hungry presence around, I felt a little more safe, and the years of molestation started becoming a memory. Maybe, just maybe, it would all be forgotten like it never happened.

My mom started attending a church that a co-worker had invited her to. After a few weeks, my mother made a huge shift in her life: she received Jesus as her Savior. Now after my mom had birthed my baby sister, her perspective began to change.

But still, up until this point, she had been a drinker, partier, and was consistently dating and getting hurt by men. After she received Christ, I started seeing her drink less and less, read her Bible, and pray.

She started taking me with her to church, and I saw things that blew my little mind. I watched people who were mentally and physically sick get healed when the pastor came and prayed for them. I would watch, amazed, as they would testify in detail of how God had healed them.

One time, the pastor called up people who needed to be healed. All of a sudden, a woman in the row across from mine fell to the floor and started slithering to the aisle of the church like a snake.

The pastor walked right up to her. "In the name of Jesus, I command you to loose her now!", he shouted.

With a scream, the woman's body convulsed, and then went limp.

I watched, intrigued, as if watching a movie. By this point, I'd become used to seeing people delivered from demons at my church, and it was always exciting. The pastor prayed for her, and when he finished, he encouraged her to stand. Slowly, shakily, she attempted to push herself up. When she was able to finally stand all the way up, she started praising God. "Come on church, let's praise God for setting her free," the pastor said

In the midst of shouts of joy, I remember looking at the pastor in amazement and thinking, *I want the Jesus he has.*

Not long after that, I started attending youth group. The

youth pastor challenged us to develop a personal relationship with Jesus. I was young and still trying to figure God out, so I didn't really know what that looked like. I also didn't know what the pastor meant when he talked about being saved and "accepted by God". All I knew was that when I was at church, I felt a welcoming warmth and a sense of community that my heart longed for. I wanted to be where God and God's people were.

One day, my mom and I were in the produce section of a grocery store and we happened to run into my pastor. My heart skipped a beat when I saw him. After seeing the change in my mom, I'd been thinking, even as a seven year-old, about praying to receive Jesus as my personal Savior. When I saw my pastor, I knew it was my moment.

While he and my mom made small talk, I mustered up the courage to open my mouth and voice my desire.

"Pastor, I want to have Jesus in my heart," I said, trying to control my nervous excitement. His face lit up, and he kneeled down. It didn't seem to matter to him that we were out in public in between the apples and bananas-he seemed proud and honored to lead me to the Lord.

He led me in a short prayer, and I repeated after him. Almost immediately, I could tell something was different. I felt lighter and happier on the inside.

Somehow, I understood that I wanted to start all over again with all the sexual mess I'd been involved in, so at that moment, I vowed to the Lord that I would keep myself pure and stay away from sex until I was married.

Worship soon became one my favorite activities. I would worship the Lord at church and then go into my bedroom and worship some more. I began to read my Bible to the best of my ability, take notes at church, and do whatever else I could to learn more about God and spend time with Him. It was evident that something had changed inside of me, because I desired to learn more about God. And the more I learned, the hungrier I became.

One night, I dreamed that I saw Jesus on His knees in prayer. He was wearing a white robe, and even in the dream I could sense His tenderness. "Jesus," I said. He reached out and He touched my shoulder. When He did, we ascended together. He began to share with me His heart for the world, and I could see the compassion in His eyes and hear the love in His voice for the people in the earth.

"Stacey, I'm broken for what the enemy has done to my deceive my people and turn them away from Me," He said. I was impacted by the tenderness in His tone, and I looked back toward the earth, where I saw young people playing. "I'm going to use you to bring many people back to Me," He said, and the dream ended.

I had this same dream multiple times, and it made my heart begin to long for the reality of who this man Jesus was. I knew that there was something bigger and greater than what I could even physically see at church, and I wanted to discover it.

Chapter 2

I CONTINUED TO FAITHFULLY ATTEND CHURCH and grow in God as much as I knew how to, but by the time I was in 8th grade, the influence of my peers at school began to pull me in. It didn't take long for me to become consumed with being popular, focusing on my personal appearance, and making friends.

I found myself with mature sexual desires for boys my age. It didn't take too much effort to find boys who were as curious and willing to explore sexual possibilities as I was. I would sneak off with them after school, in between classes, on field trips, during band practice, and any other time I could. Every sexual encounter always left me hungry for more, and I could feel an insatiable desire for sexual pleasure brewing and growing in me.

Although I remembered my vow to the Lord, at this point,

I felt that I was staying faithful to my end of the promise as long as I didn't do the "real thing". So I continued to do sexual things, and when I didn't have access to a person, I would masturbate. Eventually, I began engaging sexually with boys in my family as well. I knew what I was doing was wrong, but I'd already become so addicted to sexual pleasure that I really couldn't stop.

Towards the end of my 8th grade year, my school band participated in a parade held in Corpus Christi, TX. I was a drummer. After the competition, as we headed back to Houston, a strange thing happened. As I stared out the window at the blur of cars, a thought crossed my mind.

Jessica is really cute.

Jessica was a girl on the dance team. I remember shifting in my seat uncomfortably, thinking, *why did I just think that? Jessica was a girl!*

But she looks really good in her dance uniform.

I couldn't believe these thoughts were coming to my mind. I glanced nervously around me at my peers, feeling very weird that I was having these thoughts right in their midst.

I continued to think about her over the next few days, and as I did, my desire for her begin to grow like a weed. I became completely obsessed and made it a point to know where she was at all times. I knew when she had science, math, cheerleading practice, and even where she got picked up after school. I still couldn't understand how sexual thoughts about a girl had entered my head and how to get rid of them. I'd never heard anyone in my church talk about these things. I wasn't sure how to process what I was thinking and feeling, and none of my friends had ever had feelings for the same sex, so I said nothing. I thought that by keeping everything inside, I could hide my struggle. Plus, I really didn't believe anyone really cared anyway.

I never acted on the thoughts or feelings I had toward Jessica, but over the course of the school year, they never left no matter how much I tried to make them. I continued to grow and cultivate an unexpressed desire for her throughout my 8th grade year, and because of this, my perspective toward myself began to change. *Who am I and what is happening to me?* I would think. I knew from reading the Bible and from what I learned in church that I was a child of God and important to Him. However, the things that were going on in my mind and emotions accused me and told me otherwise.

The next school year, I entered high school. I never figured out how to deal with the crazy thoughts about Jessica, so within just a few short months, I started actually entertaining thoughts of having relationships with girls. I didn't dare act on them, but daily, hour after hour, I would roll thoughts and scenarios through my mind. I would think continuously on sexual possibilities and potential girlfriend/girlfriend situations, and every thought made the sexual monster inside me grow.

This school year was different. Because I'd worked hard in the summer to develop my basketball and drumming skills,

I gained popularity and more students wanted to talk to me. The girls' basketball team began to embrace me and include me in their "circle". I began to hear them gossip about other people and about how they thought so-and-so was cute. And it wasn't long before somebody finally popped the question.

"Hey Stacey, have you ever thought about messing around with girls?"

I was shocked. *Was it that obvious?* It was like they knew. These girls were so open about their sexuality that although I wasn't willing to confess my recently developed obsession with girls, their openness drew me in and made me feel almost comfortable with it. I'd never before encountered a group of people so confident about who they were.

I eventually discovered that half the team was either lesbian or bisexual and proud of it. During practices, in the locker room, and on buses, they'd freely talk inappropriately about both guys and girls. Their confidence was magnetic, but I still couldn't bring myself to share anything personal. I felt safer if my struggles were hidden in my own soul, away from judgmental ears.

As weeks turned into months, I found that hiding this much confusion and sexual desire in my mind was not as safe as I thought. I even tried being in a relationship with one of the guys at my school, but after awhile it was obvious that it wasn't going to work out. During the end of the relationship I found myself once again thinking about other girls.

Constantly thinking lustful thoughts built up such strong

desires in me that I was constantly in a state of overwhelm. I also felt helpless, because who was going to understand a ninth-grade church girl who had same-sex attractions?

For the rest of that basketball season, the team tried to put pressure on me to admit my sexual involvements, but I didn't give in. I tried my best to hide the fact that I was really intrigued and drawn in by the lesbian lifestyle. I continued to wear skirts and tight clothes as a disguise, hoping that my peers and my mom wouldn't be able to see past my outer facade.

However, anyone who understands the way thoughts work knows that you can't just keep sowing them and not expect them to, at some point, bear fruit. Eventually, my physical appearance started reflecting what was going on in my mind. I was becoming stronger athletically, and I started walking with the type of swag that the dudes my age had. After a while, day by day, it became obvious that I wasn't a typical girl, and other students started questioning me about my sexuality.

"Do you have a girlfriend?"

"How long have you been turned out?"

They weren't asking me these things to find out whether or not I was a lesbian. They asked me these things because they *assumed* I was a lesbian and wanted to know was how many girls I'd been sexually involved with. I would shrug them off, never responding. I was still determined to be completely internal about it all, but the pressure to be open and expressive was undeniably mounting. I could tell that sooner or later I'd have to come out as a full-fledged lesbian or else I'd blow over.

Meanwhile, I secretly started nurturing a relationship with a girl named Destiny from the previous school I attended. It started out as just a friendship, and we were in constant communication. As we continued to communicate, however, I began to develop passions and emotions that were outside the appropriate bounds of a female friendship. It didn't take long for our conversations to go from favorite foods, favorite colors, and favorite music, to family, goals, and inevitably, sexuality.

"I have a question for you Stacey, and I'm not trying to be weird," she said one day.

"Ok, go ahead."

"Have you ever been in a relationship with another girl?"

I froze and my mouth went dry. It was as if that single question activated all the passions I'd been cultivating, and it was almost too much emotion for one moment. My stomach fluttered and I could feel lust stirring. Still, I was too scared to be open, so I dodged the question.

"With other girls? I never really thought about that," I lied.

Every conversation we had after that began to slowly weaken my ability to mask my passions. I could tell that it was only a matter of time before everything was going to come flooding out.

The same week Destiny probed my interest in same sex attractions, a teammate of mine cornered me before practice.

"So Stacey, you ever been with a girl?" she asked. I could tell by the look in her eyes that she already assumed I had and was pulling at an admission.

Again, I was able to dodge the question and end the conversation. I couldn't believe it. Twice in the same week I'd been asked the same question. It seemed as if circumstances were intentionally lining up to present me to the world as a full-fledged homosexual. With every conversation, I began to be more and more comfortable with the lesbian lifestyle.

Strangely, I also suddenly began to gain a lot of attention from girls both on the basketball team and at school. One particular girl and I both began expressing our attraction toward one another, and I quickly became addicted to her. I constantly spent time on the internet or the phone with her every opportunity I had. Over a matter of weeks, our conversations began to solidify our relationship, and eventually we decided that we didn't want to keep "sugar coding" our conversations. We wanted to make our relationship public (at least at school, anyway).

At this point, the internal pressure and passion was already overflowing, and I couldn't hold it in any longer. I was finally ready to go all in and fully embrace the lesbian lifestyle publicly.

I didn't make a big announcement to my friends and family because I didn't want questions or opposition. But there was a big shift in my perspective and in my heart from this point on. This was who I truly was and what I wanted to be.

I tried my best to keep everything hidden, as much as possible, from my mom. But all moms have a special "mom sense" about their children, and I could tell she was growing suspicious. One day I was on the phone with the girl I was dating at the time, but I had to run to band practice. As I got off the phone with her I didn't say "I love you" just in case my mom was close enough to hear me, so I waited to text it when I hung up the phone.

In the rush of leaving the house for band practice, I accidently left the phone on my bed. I was halfway to school before I realized I didn't have it.

"Man! I left my phone home!" I said, trying to hide my panic. "Can you turn around?"

"Nope," my mom replied coolly. From her response, I knew that she would find my phone, read through my texts, and that would be it for me.

During band practice that day, I couldn't focus. I was thinking about how I was going to lie my way out of this situation. After one of our water breaks, my band director called me in the office and told me to get my stuff ready because my mother was on her way due to a "family emergency". My stomach immediately dropped and fear spread over me like a current. *Oh no. She must have read my texts,* I thought. I honestly hoped that there was an actual family emergency, but in my heart of hearts, I knew there wasn't.

My mother picked me up from practice and acted completely normal as we were driving away from school. We pulled up to my favorite Mexican restaurant and I tried to force-calm my shaky nervousness. We ordered our food and carried on like everything was normal. After a while, I began to think that maybe she genuinely just wanted to have lunch with me and that maybe she hadn't read anything on my phone after all. I began to relax and enjoy my beans and rice.

Until she popped the question.

"So who's the young lady that messaged you and said she loved you?" she asked.

I was caught off guard. "She's just a friend. We always say that to each other," I tried to lie casually.

"Well why does she love you? Do you love her?"

"No, Mom, we don't love each other like that," I said, forcing a light chuckle. I'd become a professional at hiding my emotions, and since she couldn't read past that response, I hoped the matter was liquidated.

We left the restaurant and I thought I had actually gotten away with the lie I told her. To play it safe, however, I told the girl I was dating what had happened, and we decided to just be friends.

Chapter 3

THIS "SCARE" OF MY MOM ALMOST FINDING OUT my secret lifestyle wasn't enough to deter me from fully embracing homosexuality, however. I wanted to go deeper into lesbianism: I wanted to actually be a student of the lifestyle.

I wanted to know all the ins and outs of being a homosexual. I wanted to know how they lived, what the lifestyle was like, and most of all, how to sexually engage other women. I spent a great deal of time watching pornography, both on video and on the internet. By the time I was finishing my sophomore year, I was not only still talking to Destiny, but I was also connecting with other young women from different schools. It was as if I had an inward magnet, and women began to come from all over. It was as if I'd discovered a whole community that had been waiting for me my whole life, a community of people who understood my desires.

It became nearly impossible to try to keep it from my mom, as day by day I was looking the part more and more. By this time, my mom had become a strong believer and a woman of prayer, so there were very few things I knew I'd be able to successfully get past her. I wasn't ready to discuss my decision with her, so I tried to stay low key as much as possible. However, during the summer between my 10th and 11th grade year, she started dating a new guy. He became her focus, so I knew I'd easily be able to get away with more than usual.

With this new man consuming her attention, it gave me the freedom to pursue my life as a homosexual without her always in my business. I was convinced that if I was a homosexual, the chances of getting pregnant, getting a sexually transmitted disease, or being hurt by a man were very slim. I'd seen my mom hurt by many men, and I wanted no part of that. I told myself that if I were to ever have a woman of my own, I would treat her better than any man could ever treat a woman. In my disillusionment, I became a broken girl on a mission to heal women.

During this time, I started treating porn like study material. Since I'd fully embraced the lesbian lifestyle, I wanted to be a lesbian who knew what I was doing.

Until this time, I had no idea porn could be accessed for free online. I watched pornography videos to learn how homosexuals actually have sex and do other things for sexual pleasure. I studied the lifestyle, the mentality behind it, and how to please women. As I continued to study, it was like something supernatural transpired in my life, and I became even more of a female magnet for homosexual women.

In spite of all this, I was still going to church, but only because it was a requirement in my household. I was still actively participating on the praise team, mime team, dance team, step team, and singing in the choir. I felt guilty all the while, and I could feel God tugging at my heart to turn back to Him. However, my mind was too invested and consumed with homosexuality. I knew what I was doing wasn't right in God's eyes, so I participated in as few ministry opportunities as possible.

Despite enjoying this new lifestyle, however, I was struggling internally. I sincerely wanted to talk to someone about what I was experiencing. I longed to be able to lay my inner struggles bare and truly receive help without getting judged. I felt that of all places, church should be the place where I could find that help, yet most Christians came off as unapproachable. As sensitive and raw as this topic was, I didn't trust anyone I knew, so I just continued to keep everything in.

I'd also never before heard of anyone successfully getting out of the homosexual lifestyle, so I assumed I was probably going to walk this path alone. It seemed that if anyone did notice me struggling, no one reached out to try to help.

Summer time was approaching, which meant I had to spend an entire month at my father's house. I hated having to go to his house every other weekend, and I cried every time. He'd never been there for me, especially when I needed him.

I didn't care that he tried to make our time together fun now.

I would make it a point to stay in my room the entire month I spent with him. I had, by this point in my life, built an invisible wall that no one, especially him, could cross. I felt safe behind this wall, and protected from any other dramatic, conflictual or potentially emotionally harmful events.

I completely avoided talking to my dad and his wife at all costs. I made it obvious that they couldn't climb the wall I built, and I was proud of it. This particular summer, I also committed myself to growing as a lesbian. When I thought no one was watching, I would get on dating and pornography websites and "study." The moment I'd finish lunch, dinner, or any other family activity, I'd head straight to the computer. I searched for any and everything related to lesbians and homosexuals such as events, support groups, shows, dating sites, and porn pages.

I didn't find out until years later that my dad had actually walked in on me one day as I was browsing. He never said anything, but I can imagine how hurtful it must have been for him.

At the time, though, I wasn't really concerned who I was hurting. All I cared about was me and this new lifestyle I was living.

Chapter 4

By the time I started 11th grade, it was well-known around school that I was a full-fledged lesbian. I expressed my sexuality freely at school and other public places, but at home and at church, I still tried to keep it hidden. When something has become a lifestyle, though, you can't hide it forever.

The only way I was able to keep it even remotely hidden from my mom was by wearing the school clothes she bought me and changing into men's clothes in the school bathroom. I secretly saved my own money to buy men's clothes. I also stole the clothes of the guy my mother was dating at the time. This man was a minister and a businessman, and after they'd dated for a while, he moved in with us. My mom would faithfully wash his clothes and I would steal them from the dryer before she could fold them. I honestly don't know how he never noticed that his clothes were gone, but if he did, he never mentioned it.

I was always ready with two pairs of clothes every day. I'd show up to school in the girly outfits my mom had purchased, and when I walked into the school building, I would head straight to the restroom to change.

At the beginning of the school year I wasn't in a steady relationship with anyone, so I involved myself with multiple girls around my school. I would go to their houses from time to time and showcase everything I'd learned the last several months of studying.

By this time, the whole basketball team knew I was gay. Most of them were homosexual as well, and they'd all flirt and mess around with one another.

One day, our team was at a tournament. During our breaks, we would watch other teams play and just sit together and hang out. Some of my teammates at this time would start to touch each other inappropriately, right there in the open. It was nerve-racking for me to see them doing that, but no was really paying attention, not even the coach.

It was during one of these break times that I all of a sudden felt someone's hand slide down my pant leg. I jumped and grabbed the hand immediately. It was one of my teammates named Danae who'd just been touching and flirting with another girl a few minutes before. I was confused, and yet I also couldn't deny the flood of sexual passion it aroused in me. I gave her a "what are you doing" look, but she paid no attention and kept touching me boldly without backing off.

Not able to withstand the sexual pressure, I started touching her back.

Our team took the floor again. The game was very close, and I wasn't playing well. I was missing easy shots I would normally make, and we ended up losing.

Now I was as equally passionate about basketball as I was about homosexuality, so when we lost, I was very upset. By the time we got on the bus, I didn't want to talk to anyone. I sat towards the back of the bus, covered my face with my blanket, and wept.

I felt one of my teammates sit next to me. I glanced up, and it was Danae. I turned away, not wanting to be bothered.

"It's ok Stacey," she said, caressing my arm. "We still have a lot more games this season." She tried hugging me but I brushed her off. She then slid her hand under my blanket and interlaced her fingers with mine. I made my hand limp, trying to get her to see that I was still upset about the game and wanted to be left alone. But she was persistent. I finally gave in and held her hand. *Why was I so easily aroused?*

Taking this as an acceptance invitation, she shoved her hand down my pants again.

I screamed at the top of my lungs, and she slapped her other hand over my mouth. My teammates and coach looked back to see what was wrong, but I didn't say anything.

"*What the heck are you doing?*" I whisper-yelled, but she just smiled. For the rest of the bus ride, she tried all sorts of touchy-feely flirtatious things until I'd had enough. "Stop for *real*," I said firmly, and she finally withdrew her hands as we pulled into the school.

As I reached down to pull out my gym bag from under my bus seat, however, she suddenly jerked my face around and drew me into a kiss. Shocked and deeply stirred, I kissed her back. Fireworks went off in my belly, and I felt butterflies like never before.

I tried to act normal when I got in my mom's car, but I was so overwhelmed with emotions and sexual thoughts that I had to either look straight ahead or out the window. It was so awkward and uncomfortable to have those images in my mind with my mom sitting next to me, and when we finally made it home, I bolted to my room, still trying to process the overwhelming emotions.

The interesting thing about Danae is that she was considered to be one of the pretty girls at school that all the guys *and* girls wanted to date. She was also dating one of the most popular guys at school. That didn't keep her away from me, however. After that encounter, she was faithful to continue to express her feelings towards me, and any moment we were alone turned sexual.

One day, we were talking on the phone and she asked a very puzzling question.

"Do you want to be my girlfriend?"

"You have a boyfriend," I responded.

"It doesn't matter," she said. "We can make it work." I didn't really know what to say, but I loved the attention she gave me

34

and I was very attracted to her. "Ok, yes," I said. It felt good to feel wanted, especially by someone so highly desired by others.

This marked the beginning of a steady sexual relationship with her. We were very crafty with our relationship. We'd act like we were just teammates when her boyfriend was around, but we took every opportunity to have all the sex we could get-before school, during school, after school, weekends, school holidays, and any time in between. By this point, I had become completely addicted to her and would lie to my mom and sneak out of the house just to be with her.

One day during chemistry, the front office came over the intercom. "Please release Astacia Jones to the main office, her mother is here to see her." As you can imagine, my heart dropped to my stomach. My mom was a teacher at another school, so I never expected her to pop up unexpectedly. I dashed to the girls' basketball locker room to change my clothes because I needed to change from my boy clothes to my "girly outfit". When I got to the office, I could tell my mom was suspicious, and she asked me what took so long.

"I had go to the restroom," I lied. She eyed me suspiciously, but handed me the keys to her car. "Drive yourself home after practice. I have to stay late to get some work done," she said. I was beyond relieved. My heart had been pounding in my chest the entire time, and I was beyond relieved that this was all she wanted. I went back to class prideful, because I thought I got away with covering up my double life.

My mother did a couple more pop-ups, but I was always

ready with my extra outfit in my bag just in case. The fact that I was continuing to get away with this sneakiness gave me confidence that I could get away with other things bigger than just wearing a boy's outfit at school.

My mom allowed me to keep the car because I'd proven myself, according to her knowledge, to be a very responsible child. I didn't want to break her trust, so I stayed on top of the things she asked me to do so that she would continue to allow me to do things I wanted to do. Because she worked far from my school, I had a lot of time to do things I wanted to do if I wasn't in basketball, band, church or dance practice. Since I now had a car, I would go get my friends food during lunch, take them home, and go to my girlfriend's house. This became the norm for me throughout the school year. With all this confidence built up, I began to take riskier moves.

I went to my girlfriend's house on a day I didn't have school and my mom was at work. While I was on the way, my girlfriend called me.

"Hey, park on the next street just in case my dad comes home so he won't see your car in the driveway," she said. When I got there, I entered the house and bounded up the stairs. After some flirting and foreplay, we lay in her bed, talking.

All of a sudden, the downstairs door opened and shut.

"Quick, get on the floor behind the bed," she whispered. I hit the floor, trying to breathe quietly even though I was pretty sure my heart sounded like a drum. I had never met her father and didn't want to now.

After a few moments she leaned over the bed. "Go through the side door and run to the car. I'm gonna stall him with a conversation. I'll see you tomorrow."

We tiptoed downstairs and when her dad turned his back to the door, she opened the door and I ran to my car like somebody was chasing me. I drove off, still huffing and puffing, promising myself I would never do that again.

Sexual ties aren't easily cast aside, however, and I found myself over at her house many more times. I was being sneaky and wasn't getting caught, which gave me boldness to continue to do risky things.

On one occasion, her mom unexpectedly came home early. Again, I hit the floor. Seconds later, my cell phone rang. *Oh just great*, I thought, as I fumbled to silence the ringer. I looked at the screen and saw that it was my mom, and I knew if I didn't answer, she'd keep calling me.

On this particular day, I was supposed to be babysitting my little sister, who was ten years old. I'd left her at home napping, figuring that I would just sneak over to Danae's house, get some sexual satisfaction, and sneak back before she woke up. Now, I was concerned that something had happened.

I picked up the phone. "Hello?" I whispered.

"Why are you whispering?" my mom asked.

"Mom, I'm not whispering," I lied, trying my best to make my voice louder.

"Girl, yes you are," she said.

I tried to lift my voice a little bit. "Can you hear me now?"

"Yes, that's better. How's Asia doing?"

"She's good, she's still asleep," I lied, hoping that my little sister hadn't woken up to see that I wasn't there. She would tattle on me for sure.

"Ok good. I'll be home in a few hours," she said, and hung up. I sighed, relieved that I was able to get her off the phone without her asking too many questions. Now my next challenge would be to get out of the house without Danae's mother seeing me. This time, my car was parked at the house across the street, so I had to figure out how to get in the car without being seen.

Danae went to the kitchen and got the trash out of the trash can, acting like she had forgotten to take it out. Her mom went in her room, and when Danae opened the door, I bolted out and didn't look back.

I made it back home in time to turn off the stove, check on my little sister, and look like I'd been there the entire time. My confidence in my ability to be deceptive and sneaky was growing, and I felt like I was slick enough to get out of any situation.

Valentine's Day came around, and I was ready to spoil Danae. I bought her a teddy bear, some chocolates, and a card expressing my love for her. I got to school early to wait for her by her locker, giddy with excitement.

As I was waiting, I paced the hallway with anticipation. After walking back and forth for a while, I turned the corner at a hallway that had another set of lockers. I froze.

There was Danae, flirting with another girl! I stared, not wanting to believe my eyes. *Was this really happening?*

Angry and hurt, I turned and stormed down the other hallway, dramatically dumped everything I'd bought her into the first trash can I saw and kept walking. I was angry at her for using me but angrier at myself for allowing myself to be used.

By the end of the day, I found out that not only was she dating me and her boyfriend, but she had five other girls she was involved with. I was so confused and hurt. *How in the world has she been hustling all these different relationships?* I wondered.

I purposely walked past her locker after school so she could see me and I could ignore her. "Stacey, wait," she called, as I walked by. She pulled the string of my backpack, but I yanked it back. I turned and looked her in the eye. "We're done," I said coolly, and kept walking.

I was depressed the rest of that school year. The only thing that kept me a little motivated about life was music and basketball. I knew in my heart that the Lord was wanting my attention, and to be honest, this would have been the perfect opportunity for me to completely turn to Him. However, I didn't see or know Him as a loving Father who really cared about me, so I felt justified in just ignoring the inner promptings I felt. With my mom focused on her boyfriend and my dad on his marriage and money, I literally had no outlet. I channeled all my anger and pain into basketball.

Chapter 5

I REALLY WANTED TO PLAY COLLEGE BASKETBALL, so my parents allowed me to attend summer trainings and leagues to improve my skills. I dedicated all my time and energy into training, but that didn't hide or heal the wounds in my heart.

Danae tried to pursue me, but I was determined not to allow her back in. I resisted all attempts at restoring our relationship and tried my best to push her out of my mind.

During the summer, my heart began to come under conviction that there was more to life than the way I was living. I couldn't explain it, but the Spirit of God was constantly trying to get my attention. I didn't want to surrender, though, because in my eyes, God cared more about me behaving than He cared about me as a person. But I also didn't want to be on His bad side, so I thought that maybe if I changed the way I dressed, He would see that I was sorry.

I began to pray and read my Bible more, thinking that

doing these things would help me to be strong when I went back to school my senior year. I was going to need strength to resist the temptation of falling for my ex-girlfriend. I bought more feminine clothing and changed my hairstyle so she would know I was serious about changing.

When I walked into the building the first day of my senior year, my peers didn't hide their surprise at the fact that I was now dressing feminine. I didn't care. I was still carrying the open wound from what Danae had done on Valentine's Day, and I was determined to change my lifestyle. No one was ever going use me like that again.

For all my good intentions, however, my "transformation" only lasted about six weeks before I was back in men's clothing and talking to girls. And for all the promises I made to myself that I'd never let Danae back in, she and I began talking again, a little at first, but as one day turned into the next, we were once again on good terms.

By the second month of school, despite my effort to be "focused on basketball," I found myself in a full-fledged relationship with Danae once again. The soul tie we had from being sexually engaged was so strong that even when I wanted to let go and do right, it felt impossible.

What I didn't know at this time of my life was that homosexuality is an intense bondage that I wasn't going to be able to break on my own. I thought that if I just changed my clothes, tried to ignore Danae, and poured myself into basketball, I'd successfully just walk out of the lifestyle of homosexuality. But I had sown too many seeds, and I wasn't rooted in the truth of God's Word, so I fell quickly into bondage again.

By this time, a lot of my church youth were now students at school, including my sister. Every day, as I drove home from school, I was on the phone, talking and flirting with girls from school. I was so caught up in myself that I didn't even realize that my little sister, who rode with me every day, was watching and observing my life.

One weekend, I had a basketball tournament and one of my teammates came over to spend the night with me because she needed a ride. Now my little sister had been telling my mom the things she'd heard me say on the phone, so my mom was suspicious. She let me have my teammate over but took away my phone.

I tried to cover myself as much as possible by deleting all my inappropriate text messages "just in case" she pried through it. I didn't delete my voicemails, though, because I liked listening to them.

About thirty minutes after my mom took my phone, she came back in my room and asked me for the password to my voicemail. I didn't know what to do. If she listened to my voicemails, I was done, but I knew she would badger me if I didn't give it to her.

When I finally gave her the code, I knew I was finished. After she walked away, I immediately borrowed my teammate's phone to call Danae.

"Hello?" she said.

"Hey Danae, we need to break up," I said immediately.

"Why?"

"Because my mom is listening to my voicemails right now and she's about to hear all the ones you've left me," I said.

"Oh my gosh Stacey! You kept those?" she asked.

"I did. I like listening to them. But we need to end our relationship now," I said.

I didn't see my mom until the next morning. As soon as I woke up, she immediately called me to her bathroom. Her demeanor told me all I needed to know.

She leaned against the counter and crossed her arms. "The first thing I wanted to do with you was send you to your father's house, but I told God I'm not going to let the devil have you. I can't believe this," she said, shaking her head, anger clearly in her eyes. "This is embarrassing to me as a mom. I will not allow you to live this way under my roof, do you understand me?"

I was silent, shielding my heart from condemnation and guilt. I tried to look repentant. She continued on and on and demanded that I break up with my girlfriend.

As I walked out of the room, I was both embarrassed and angered. Embarrassed, for obvious reasons. But angered because I was hurting on the inside and she couldn't, and didn't try to, see it.

At church that Sunday, the pastor set aside time for anyone who wanted prayer at the end of the service. My mom grabbed my hand and said, "Let's go get prayer". I really didn't want to go, because she was forcing me. But I was too scared of God to say no to prayer, so I went.

What my mom didn't understand is that I truly *wanted* to feel and live differently. I didn't like the confusion, the hurt, and the turmoil I constantly felt on the inside. On the other hand, I also enjoyed the sexual pleasure that came with the lesbian lifestyle. When we got to the altar, I could feel the presence of God, and a Spirit-flesh battle started within me.

The ministers at the altar prayed for me and to be honest, I wasn't concerned with them or what they were praying. I just really wanted some type of change. When they finished praying, I started thinking about how this would play out in real life. *How in the world am I gonna do this?* I thought. I'd have to get rid of my clothes, friends, phone numbers, and anything that had to do with that lifestyle. Just the thought of that was overwhelming.

The ministers who prayed for me asked me to come to the back of the church. Immediately, my walls went up. The last thing I wanted was to be cornered.

"Go ahead and sit right here, Stacey," one of the ministers said. "We just really wanted to call you back here to, you know, just minister to you and to let you know that you're beautiful just the way you are. God made you unique and special, and He has a special calling on your life."

"Yes," the other minister chimed in, "and you don't need to live or dress like a man. Why is it that you feel a need to do so?"

I stayed in that office almost an hour, mainly listening,

as they talked in circles about why I "felt the need" to be a lesbian. After I left that meeting and was walking out, another minister pulled me aside.

"You know, it's possible to wear baggy clothes and still make them look feminine. There are plenty of female celebrities who dress like this, and they still look like ladies."

"Thanks," I said, biting back tears.

I left church that evening feeling more confused, overwhelmed, and unfinished. I was given a lot of information on what to do and what not to do, yet the feelings, desires and uncertainties were still there. I was really battling between the desire to be free and the very addicting pleasures of the homosexual lifestyle.

That evening I sat in my room feeling hopeless, lost, and having no idea what to do next. I knew I couldn't have been the only person in the world who wanted freedom, but I had no one to reach out to for insight and direction, no one to guide me with day-to-day instructions or walk me through to healing and wholeness. My only ray of hope was to connect with someone at the new Christian college I'd be attending in the fall. Surely this was my opportunity to get away, find some help, and start fresh.

I hoped beyond hope that this new door would lead me into a new life.

Chapter 6

WHEN I STEPPED FOOT ON THE CAMPUS of Dallas Christian College as a freshman, my heart was filled with excitement at the promise of newness all around me. There were many opportunities to connect with leaders and ministers, as well as weekly chapels to attend. Unlike the atmosphere I'd just come out of, there seemed to be help everywhere I turned, and I was more than ready to receive it.

I made the basketball team, so I decided that the best place to start looking for freedom would be to reach out to the leadership on my team. Reaching out to someone closer to my age seemed the best and most comfortable route to take, so I asked to meet with one of the captains after practice one afternoon in the dorm.

When she came, we began to talk about our different life experiences and how we each came to know the Lord. She shared with me some challenges she'd faced in her life, and to my surprise, they were very similar to my own experiences. I got excited because I felt that this was going to be my moment to find out how to be truly free and renew my life in Christ again.

"You know, there's something that I've really been struggling with and I think you may be able to help me," I said, opening up. "A couple years ago, I fully embraced the homosexual lifestyle. I've been intimate with girls for a while now, and part of me really likes it, but at the same time, deep down I really want to be free from it. I just don't know how to get there."

She raised her eyebrows, and for a split second I thought I had shared too much.

"That's crazy that you mention that, Stacey," she said, lowering her voice. "I've honestly had that same struggle, and I've felt the same thing: it's like I like it, but at the same time something in me is crying out to get free."

Tears sprang to my eyes. I wanted to cry and hug her. For the first time in my life, I found someone who truly understood me. She invited me to hang out with the team later that evening, and I gladly accepted her invitation. I entrusted myself to her because I thought she'd be my ticket out of this mental torment.

Later that evening, I was in the car with four of my teammates. "Where are we going?" I asked as I buckled my seatbelt. I was so full of hope and excitement I could hardly contain myself. "You'll see," the driver, a point guard, said, with a twinkle in her eye.

Twenty minutes later, we pulled into the parking lot of what looked like a nightclub. "What is this place?" I asked.

"What do you think?" one of my teammates answered, smiling. "It's a gay nightclub!"

"A what?" I asked, not fully comprehending what she said.

I stared, open-mouthed, at the people I saw walking in. My heart sank. I had thought we were going to some kind of church service, or maybe even just a restaurant for some team bonding. *A gay nightclub?* I thought. This couldn't be happening!

When I reluctantly walked in, I was beyond blown away. Hundreds of homosexuals, lesbians, and drag queens were everywhere, drinking and smoking and dancing. They looked and acted as if they had no care in the world but to live this lifestyle. My teammates immediately ordered drinks and headed to the dance floor.

I slumped into a seat at a table. My mind was racing with thoughts and emotions I couldn't really process, and I was disappointed and disheartened. This was the biggest upset of my life thus far, because I had made myself vulnerable about my internal battle for the first time ever, genuinely expecting to be helped. Now, I was dumped into the worst environment possible in a vulnerable state.

After an hour or so went by, I noticed an attractive woman sitting at the bar drinking a beer. She was staring straight at me, boldly. After a few minutes of this, I started to get nervous.

Does she want to fight me? Is she into me? I thought. I wasn't sure, so I did my best to avoid her gaze.

By the time the last song of the night came on, I had loosened up a bit and had forcefully put aside my disappointment. I decided to get on the dance floor. Almost immediately, the lady at the bar came over and unashamedly started dancing on me. I was a little surprised, but I danced with her until the song ended. As my teammates were getting ready to leave, she and a few other girls followed us to the car. By this time, I had purposely ignored my convictions and was once again full-on focused on the homosexual passions that were re-awakened. We had a game the next day and had to be ready early in the morning but getting back to our dorms and resting was the last thing on our minds. Instead, we decided to go to a restaurant close to the college and hang out with our new friends.

After a few hours, we exchanged numbers and finally headed home. As I lay in bed that night, I replayed the events of the evening in my head. *Maybe I shouldn't try to get free,* I thought. *After all, it seems like this comes so easily to me.*

Unbeknownst to me, that night would be the first of many times my teammates and I would end up at the gay club.

Smoking and drinking became a norm for us, as well as waking up in strangers' houses. I continued to talk to the girl from the bar at the club, and within a few weeks we became physical.

One Sunday morning, I woke up in her bed. As soon as I saw the daylight outside, I jumped up and grabbed my phone to check the time. "Oh no!" I whispered. I was still playing drums at my church, and I was supposed to have left already.

I called my pastor to let him know I wouldn't be there that morning. When I hung up, I put my head in my hands. I was partying on Saturdays and playing the drums on Sunday at a church every week. I knew I needed to change, but I didn't know how.

Being consumed with basketball, partying, girls, music, and work inevitably took its toll on my grades, and by the end of the semester, I found myself with a 1.81 GPA. It seemed like I was going downhill steadily, despite the Christian environment I was in. I attended chapel regularly, but only because it was a requirement. I never really paid attention, however, so I benefitted very little.

One day, one of the chapel speakers started talking about how the power of God has the ability to bring you out of anything. She shared how she was sexually abused and had become a lesbian for many years until she found Jesus.

For the first time in a chapel service, my attention was sparked. As she was speaking, I again felt that small ray of hope rising that I could be free, and I listened to her intently. Maybe, just maybe, she would be the one to help me settle the inner turmoil.

As she kept talking, the hope within me kept growing, and I found myself on the edge of my seat.

"Jesus did a great work in me," she said, closing her sermon. "But it took me ten years to fully be delivered."

I sunk back into my seat, discouraged. *Ten years?* I couldn't wait that long to be free. How could I even be faithful to Jesus for that long?

I left chapel feeling both hopeful and helpless. She had given me more hope than anyone I'd ever met, because I'd never heard of anyone else being delivered. But the ten-year thing seemed impossible. If Jesus was really all powerful, why did the process take so long?

Her testimony did stir me, though, so I decided to try being transparent with someone one more time. This time, I wanted to reach out to my own mom for help. She had become a strong woman of prayer, and I had come to respect her as a woman of God. So after some mental preparation, I called her. On this particular day, I was overwhelmed with emotions and feelings of being misunderstood, but I took a chance at being vulnerable. I drove to the park, which had become my go-to place when I needed to get away.

"Hey baby," my mom said, answering her phone almost immediately.

"Hey Mama," I said, not sure where to start.

She sensed my hesitancy. "What's wrong?"

I sighed. "Mom, I honestly don't know where to start. I'm so confused and I don't know what to do. I really miss Danae, but I want to be free and all of this is just so hard and confusing," I said. I went on to explain the challenge of wanting out of this lifestyle and yet feeling so stuck.

When I finished talking, I noticed that I felt a little lighter.

It felt good to get everything off my chest and be vulnerable. There was a pause at the other end, and then my mom laughed lightheartedly.

"Girl, you're going to be ok. You are fine," she responded. My heart sank. I was hoping to receive some kind of comfort, some kind of hope, or some kind of help. I felt even more hopeless, because if my own mom couldn't even understand me, who would?

That's it, I said to myself. *I'm never trying to open up about this again. I'm done.* I decided I was gonna just pour myself into the things I loved: working out, basketball, drumming, and shopping. So I did, for the next few months, until I became so numb that I hardly cared about anything.

By my second year of college, I'd worked so hard that I became one of the top scorers and actually set a record for most rebounds in a game. I practiced both before and after practice, intent on being better and better. With such a great improvement in my personal game, I began to look for other colleges to attend because I felt like there were bigger and better basketball opportunities for me elsewhere. Oddly, I also began to do a lot of thinking about marriage. I thought it would be good just to get away and get married to Danae. I was so convinced this would make me happy that I even searched the Bible for Scriptures to approve same-sex marriages. For some reason, I thought I'd be able to find biblical backing for homosexuality.

I also began to look up the process of getting a hormone

change and what I would need to do to transform into a man. I wanted to grow facial hair also, so I even began to shave parts of my face so that more hair could grow back. I figured if maybe I got surgery and a sex change it would make me feel more at peace with my desire for women.

I told the Lord in my heart that I was going to move to California, get married to Danae for five years, and come back to live my life fully for Him. This seemed like a good plan to me, so I started looking for a ring. I was serious about my decision, and I was determined that no one was going to stop me.

Little did I know that in 24 hours, my whole life would change.

PART II

Chapter 7

By this time, it was December 31, 2007, and I'd just finished the first semester of my sophomore year. A college friend invited me to his family's house for a New Year's Eve party. After a great time of celebrating with lots of food, drinks, and games, we headed home.

"Hey Stace, you look tired. Want me to drive?" my friend asked.

"Please," I said. I remember buckling my seatbelt and leaning my head on the cold door. It was way past midnight and I was tired and tipsy.

I didn't even know I'd drifted off until I opened eyes and saw a car headed straight toward us at full speed.

I bolted upright immediately. "Hey lookout!" I yelled. All I could do was stare. I glanced up at the stoplight.

Then everything went black.

When I finally became conscious, I was in a daze. My mouth was throbbing with pain, and I realized my tooth had pierced my tongue. I looked over at my friend and he seemed to be okay.

I carefully got out of the car to check on the driver of the other car. A woman raced over to me. "Are you ok?" she asked. "The other driver isn't hurt but he started throwing away all of his drugs and alcohol as soon as he got out," she said.

I eyed the other driver. It was apparent that he'd been drinking and driving, and he looked terrified. He obviously knew he could be facing some serious charges. When we realized that none of us were seriously injured, we called the police and reported the wreck.

While we were waiting, I sat on the edge of the sidewalk and tried to wrap my mind around what had just happened. It was so surreal that it was hard to believe it had actually happened. I knew in my heart that my life had been spared and that family could have easily been put in the position of having to prepare for a funeral. I looked down at my legs and feet, which hadn't been affected. I was overwhelmed. At the very least, I knew I could have easily lost the ability to ever play basketball again.

I rose to take pictures of the vehicle. As I examined the extent of the damage, reality started to sink in and my heart started to pound with anxiety. *I had just been in a major car wreck.* It was so much, too much, to handle. Had this really just happened?

I wanted to call my mom, but I knew she'd be frightened. I decided to put that off until the next day. When the police arrived, the witnesses were quick to let them know that the other driver was drinking and driving. The police gave him the number test. When he failed, he was taken away in the police car. He hung his head as they put handcuffs on him, knowing he was going to have to pay big time for his decision.

After everything was said and done, I remember lying in bed that night, unable to sleep, my mind swirling. Thoughts were racing a thousand miles per hour and everything was so foggy. It was too much to process to think that I could have actually died that night and would have entered eternity. *Where would I have really gone?* I wondered. This thought sent chills through my whole body.

The only injury I walked away with was a pierced tongue. I wasn't living for God, wasn't walking with Him, but I knew that somehow, He had spared my life.

The next morning, I called my mom.

"Hi mom," I said, trying to sound calm.

"Hey baby," she said, yawning. "How you doin?"

"Well...", I took a deep breath. I carefully explained the details of the previous night. My mom flipped and raised her voice.

"ARE YOU SERIOUS? Baby, oh my gosh...are you ok? Oh my gosh...".

She asked me more questions than I can even remember, and I couldn't really talk a lot because of the pain in my mouth.

But what I said was enough to make her fly down the highway from Houston to Dallas.

It took about three days for my mouth to heal. One morning, I was brushing my teeth and I had a strange feeling on the inside of me, like something deep was stirring. Instinctively, I had a sense that God wanted to speak to me.

I focused my mind on Him, and almost immediately, I heard His voice clear within my heart.

Stacey, who are you going to serve?

I didn't have to question what that meant. I'd served my own desires my whole life, and it ended me up in more heartbreak and emptiness than I could have ever imagined. I knew it was time for me to make a clear decision. Then He said,

She will be the death of you.

I knew exactly who and what He was talking about. "She" was my Danae, my ex, the woman I was planning to marry and give my entire life to.

It felt like I was at a crossroads. These were some serious statements, and I knew this would mean major life changes. I wanted time to think these things through before I answered the Lord.

During this time, I received a letter from my college notifying me of suspension due to a low GPA. I saw clearly how I was starting to reap the consequences of my own choices. I'd almost lost my life, I lost my car, and now I lost the opportunity to play basketball and attend college. With no other options and nowhere else to turn, I decided to move back to Houston with my mom.

My mom made it clear that I was going to continue my education no matter what, so I got a job and enrolled in community college. What God spoke to me that morning was still constantly on my heart, and I knew I needed to make a decision soon. So in the following weeks, I did a lot of thinking. I thought about my first decision to be a lesbian and how I thought that's who I really was. I thought about my ex-girlfriend and my desire to marry her, which wasn't completely gone. I thought about my excitement when I first stepped on campus, thinking I was going to find freedom. And I thought about how my life had been spared.

Something inside me was pulling for me to completely surrender my life to God. I knew it, I felt it, and oddly enough, I wanted it. So without a church service or an altar or a special song, I knelt in my bedroom, lifted my hands, opened my heart, and fully gave my life to the One who had saved it. As I closed my eyes, I could feel the presence of God washing over me, and I wept.

I knew that the emptiness that accompanied the homosexual lifestyle wasn't what He wanted for me, and that there was a better hope in Him. "I surrender, God," I whispered, tears streaming down my cheeks. I stayed in that place until I felt resolved. "God, I will do whatever you want me to do," I said. "But I will not marry a man." My mother's history with men had taught me all I needed to know, and I was determined I wouldn't walk the same path.

The first thing I did was delete phone numbers. I knew none of my friends would understand, but I knew that making a commitment to God was serious. I couldn't play around anymore.

For the first couple of months I cried myself to sleep every night. This was real. Too real sometimes. I could no longer flirt with girls or get sexual pleasure when I wanted to, and it plunged me into a state of withdrawal. Some nights were easier than others, but the thoughts, the memories, and the sexual desires that surfaced constantly threatened my decision to be free.

Sometimes I'd get so frustrated and angry, I wanted to rescind my commitment and follow the passions of my flesh. Other times I'd feel helpless and fearful, like I was alone to deal with the weight of everything. It was like finally sitting still and allowing God to deal with me caused a purging and cleansing of all the things that had been suppressed for so long. But there was no more running now, no more hiding behind homosexuality to cover what I was starting to see was the root of it all: a little broken girl, wounded and filled with insecurity.

I wanted so badly to talk to someone who had walked down this path before, someone who had been where I was and got out of it. But no matter where I looked, I could find no one. My mom tried her best to love and help me during this time, but I needed more than her "churchy" answers to my issues.

The hardest thing of all was that I couldn't find a soul in the church to make myself vulnerable to. In fact, all the Christians I knew treated me as if I had a disease, and I even overheard one leader in my church tell her daughter not to come around me or talk to me. I continued to dutifully attend church, but I knew I wouldn't find healing there.

I was so desperate to get help, I turned to the internet. Much to my surprise, I discovered accounts of other individuals who had been delivered from the homosexual lifestyle. I started learning that freedom could actually be real for me, and that I needed deliverance from the seeds that had been planted in my soul from sexual encounters at such a young age.

Daily, I read about artists, speakers, or just normal people who had been set free from the bondage and lifestyle of homosexuality. My confidence and hope grew as I read, and I was encouraged to seek God for my own deliverance.

Day by day, I began to see progress. I began to see my desire for change increase, and I could see myself free and walking in purity. Some days it was a struggle, while other days seemed to be filled with hope and small victories. I still got approached by random women wanting to see how far they could go. Some of them pretended they wanted to be friends, just to see if I'd give in to temptation, but my heart's commitment to God always prevailed.

I began to realize that I was going to have to completely reconstruct my mind if I was going to experience a new life in Christ. For six years I'd lived like a man, thought like man, walked like a man, hung around men, and had wanted to be a man. I needed to be re-trained on how to be a female. I decided to be intentional no matter what it took, and I was willing to embrace the process because I wanted real transformation.

Slowly but surely, I was starting to see how seeking God was bringing about a newness in me, and I was ready to deal with two things He was making clear needed to be dealt with: lust and perversion.

Chapter 8

I was starting to get a small taste of freedom, and it made me hungry for more. However, because of the amount of time I'd spent investing in sexual perversion, I was still struggling with masturbation and perverted thinking. I'd spent years watching pornography, masturbating, and having sex, so lust had become a part of both my frame of thinking and my personality.

I was learning how to bring my mind and my body into alignment with the Word of God and the Spirit of God, and I started doing this on a daily, weekly, and monthly basis. I was seeing small victories every day, but I still faced a lot of discouragement. Condemnation haunted me like a predator, making me feel like God was displeased with me if my mind started to wander.

However, I begin to realize that I was getting stronger

spiritually. Sins that I'd struggled with in the past were losing their hold over me and couldn't "control" me because of the strength of the Holy Spirit.

I started becoming very aware of and picky about the music I listened to, the movies I watched, and the people I hung around with, even if they professed to be Christians. These things were vital things I knew I needed to do to further my healing and deliverance.

As I continued to stay faithful in seeking the Lord, going to school, and working, opportunities began to open up for me. Without my knowledge, my mom had contacted another college basketball coach at a different university. She wanted, just as much as I did, for me to be able to continue my college basketball career.

After a while, I began to receive letters from this particular university in the mail, and I was beyond elated! I had been asking God for another opportunity to play basketball, promising that this time, I'd commit it all to Him. I had also prayed for another opportunity to experience university life. This time, though, I specifically asked the Lord to surround me with a group of friends who wholeheartedly loved Him and were people of prayer.

It seemed that God was hearing and answering this prayer, and it was almost unreal. However, I was still not academically qualified to gain admission. I was concerned, but I knew God could make it possible. So I filled out the admission application and sent my transcripts in by faith, hoping for the best.

Within a few weeks, I received a letter of acceptance! I knew that this was absolutely nothing but the favor of my Father in Heaven. Shortly after that, I also received a commitment letter to play basketball. This was unbelievable. The God I'd neglected for so long was showering undeserved blessings on my life as *if I had never even sinned against Him.* Joy began to fill my heart like I never experienced before, and somehow, I knew that this was just a taste of what it was like to walk with Him.

Chapter 9

As I made the drive from Houston to Waxahachie, Texas for the fall semester at my new university, I was almost in disbelief that this was actually happening. *I feel like I'm dreaming,* I thought. It just seemed too good to be true. After the mess of a life I'd lived, I was getting an opportunity to start all over.

I worshipped and prayed my way to the campus, fully preparing my heart for the rubber to meet the road. I was aware that I was going to have to implement the things I'd learned from God during the months I'd spent alone with Him. Even though this was a Christian university, I knew that if the other college had students who weren't completely surrendered to God, this one was bound to have some as well. I was prepared to confront anyone who wanted to try me.

At first, many people assumed I was a lesbian. I was quiet,

so I was also often misunderstood as being mean or prideful. But there were other students who clearly possessed the love God within them and embraced me. These students showed me love and acceptance that I'd only experienced in the homosexual community.

This school had an environment perfectly crafted for young adults wanting to grow in God. Daily chapel attendance was required, as were weekly dorm devotionals. The first chapel service I attended was like no other. I remember feeling the presence of God so strong that it made me weep. The message was convicting, and it stirred in me a deeper hunger to pursue God.

Being on the basketball team here was also completely different. This team loved and wanted to pursue God, and the level of support they had for one another was like I'd only experienced in the homosexual community. We went to chapel together, read the Bible, prayed, and hung out all the time with one another. Each player had her own walk with God, and we were all there for each other.

My coach and I decided that it would be best for me to red-shirt during my first year so that I could pull my GPA up without losing years of eligibility to play. He allowed me to continue to work out with the team and travel with them, but my main focus was on bringing my grades up, training, and adjusting to the expectations and culture of the university. The team didn't look at me any differently, though; they continued to love and embrace me.

I felt like I was living a dream every day, and I was so thrilled and thankful to see just how much I'd changed in less than a year. However, I still struggled with masturbation. Starving my sexual appetite completely had driven me to take pleasure in my own self, and I didn't know how to stop.

I had come to a place where the issues in my soul were beyond my personal ability to handle them. So I begin to seek help from both adults and friends that were on and off the college campus. I talked to professors, mentors, peers, and other adults I knew. Some told me masturbation was ok, while others told me that it wasn't. It was quite confusing. I knew that there could only be one right answer, so I began praying and searching the Bible for myself. I truly wanted to live with a pure conscience before the Lord and not by my own selfish desires.

I finally came to the conclusion that masturbation was wrong, and became convinced that with God's help, I could overcome it. With this wisdom, I decided I wouldn't waiver back and forth anymore. I prayed and asked forgiveness for masturbating, and I asked God to deliver me and set me free from the bondage of lust.

As we approached basketball season, I found that I was becoming more disciplined in every area of my life. Even my grades, which had been a weak point my whole life, began to exceed beyond what I ever thought possible. I was also becoming so physically fit that I could seriously play and compete with college level male athletes.

However, the fact that my life was heading in a better direction didn't mean I was exempt from traps and temptations. It was as if the devil wanted to test my resolve and my commitment to God. In the first two months of school, both males and females tried to test my boundaries and see where they could get with me. People didn't know whether to perceive me as straight or gay because I didn't dress extremely feminine, but I also didn't dress masculine. There were very attractive guys who were genuinely interested in me and there were others who just wanted sexual pleasure. However, because I was so focused on God, school, and basketball, I held my ground. I wanted nothing to with distractions.

On one occasion, I was on the phone with my mom and one of my friends walked in my room. Lounging on the couch, I motioned to her that I'd be done talking in a minute. She sauntered toward me, planting herself purposely on my lap. I stood up quickly, nearly dropping her on the floor, and walked straight out of my room. When I ended the conversation, I didn't re-enter my room. I knew she was waiting, but I didn't trust myself to respond correctly just yet.

When I finally calmed myself down, I walked back into the room, masking my frustration. She looked sheepish. "I'm so sorry," she said. "I didn't mean to make you upset."

"I know you may not have realized what you were doing, but you need to understand that this was my life for a long time," I explained. "I've been delivered from a lot, and I'm serious about my walk with Christ." She apologized again, looking ashamed, and left quickly.

For a while, I separated myself from her. I'm sure I even came across rude, because we no longer hung out, and I would only briefly greet her in passing. My walls were completely up against her because I felt that her intentions had been for me to fall.

In the midst of this situation, I realized that one of the challenges people have with cutting ties is the ability to walk away and not look back. One of the speakers I heard in chapel said to "stop flirting with your past and marry your destiny." I liked the freedom I was already tasting, and I wanted even more, so I learned to start getting comfortable with cutting things off. But even that didn't stop the enemy from throwing temptations at me on a consistent basis. Every now and then, Danae would call me. I wouldn't answer, so she would try calling from different numbers. I was always having to stay on guard.

One day after leaving the cafeteria, a friend of mine invited me to a weekly prayer meeting he was leading on campus. When I walked in, I saw a group of college students worshiping, praying, and crying out to God with passion. You could feel the intensity in the atmosphere, and you could tell every person in the room was consumed with desire for God. There was singing, clapping, dancing, crying, and at one point, students began to pray for one another.

During the meeting, a guest speaker came and spoke to the students. She was well-dressed and came across as very perceptive. When she finished speaking, she started praying for the students. As she began to pray, she also began to prophesy. I was floored again. She knew particular sicknesses that ran in student's families, dates and times that things happened, and other details. When she got to me, she prayed a simple prayer, asking God to remove insecurities and to take me deeper in my relationship with Him. By the end of the night, I was overwhelmed with what I had encountered in the meeting, between the passion of so many other students like me and the power of prophecy.

As I went to bed that night, I knew something had changed inside of me. All of a sudden, my heart longed to pray more and have a deeper walk with God, just like she'd prayed. I set my alarm clock for 5:00 the next morning, not knowing if I'd actually get up, but my spirit was hungry to spend more time in the presence of God.

When my alarm went off the next morning, I pulled myself out of bed and went to the campus prayer room. It felt so good, so productive, to be up and seeking God early in the morning. The prayer room was empty, so I sat down, leaning up against a pillar, and focused my mind on God. For the next hour, I worshipped, wept, and petitioned God, and by the time I left, I had insight, joy, and confidence. *I want this every day*, I remember thinking. From that day forward, I purposed in my heart to wake up every day and give myself to the Father before starting the day.

Now before I arrived on campus, I had prayed a small prayer

asking God to put me around people of prayer. I don't think I really understood what I was praying at the time, but the Holy Spirit must have led this prayer. I knew it was God's mercy and grace that I received my acceptance letter, but I also knew I needed friends who knew God to be in my circle. I continued to meet many others who loved to pray. I met a man of God from Haiti, and another one from the Congo. When I say these people could pray, I mean they knew how to get ahold of God and press in until something changed. Their passion was so real, and it made me hungry to really know God.

As I continued to spend time with them, I realized that I had to unlearn some things I'd picked up in church. There were concepts concerning God and rituals that I thought I had to do in order to get God's attention. Over the next few months, my capacity to pray began to grow and I found myself always talking to God. Between basketball, classes, and prayer, my time during my first year was completely taken up. I was either in class, the library, basketball practice, in the gym doing personal workouts, spending time with God or at a prayer meeting.

I was so excited to pray with my friends that I would go to prayer meetings even when I was sick. I didn't want to miss out! One evening I had the flu, but I still didn't want to miss prayer. I showed up, very weak, but I began to pray and worship. During prayer, one of my friends called me up and started praying for me. When I told him I didn't feel well, he began to pray in faith over me to be healed. As he prayed, I started to feel pain in my stomach like I'd never experienced before. The pain began to rise up to my chest and then I started to sweat as if I'd run a mile. The pain was so bad that I couldn't stand and had to bend over, putting my hands on my knees. After he finished praying for me, all of the flu symptoms were gone, and my clothes were wet from sweating. It was as if I had sweat the flu completely out. I left that prayer meeting completely healed from the flu and became even more aware of the power God.

The school year was about to end, which meant I had to go back home where most of my temptations were. Just the thought of going back home made me anxious. I didn't want all I'd experienced and overcome to be wasted.

Chapter 10

I KNEW IN ORDER TO MAINTAIN MY FREEDOM and walk with Christ, I was going to have to be disciplined, even without people of prayer there to encourage me. I carefully constructed a strategic plan to help me maintain the freedom I'd already gained.

At the beginning of summer break, I designed and started to implement my plan with focus, and even my mom and family started to notice a difference in me. I woke up earlier in the morning, spent time with God, worked out, and then went to work. I made deliverance and growth a priority. There were moments of weakness where I fell short with pornography and masturbation, and I would feel so ashamed. I would feel condemned and unworthy to talk to God.

One day, it dawned on me that there was a pattern to my actions. I realized I was being enticed and drawn in to sin, and then made to feel condemned afterward. I learned that it was the enemy's job to both tempt and condemn. He was the one tempting me to commit the sin and was right there to condemn me when I did it. When I understood that he was on both sides of the sin, I began to look at temptation and sin from a completely new perspective, and it strengthened my ability to resist.

While I wasn't actively watching porn or masturbating, I could constantly feel the temptation to do so. But the more and more I resisted the temptation, the stronger I felt myself becoming. I still had moments of weakness where I would give in, but when that would happen, I'd make it a point to change settings, go workout, or pray. I did the best I knew how to do to guard my heart as much as possible.

I was already prepared for the fact that my growing freedom wasn't going unnoticed and wasn't going to be unchallenged by the powers of darkness. But this time, I had enough knowledge of Satan and his kingdom to know that he'd try to use whatever he could from my past to attempt to pull me back in.

I was right.

Danae called me, and not just once. She called so many times I started second-guessing myself. *Maybe something bad happened to her,* I thought. I let the phone go to voicemail for a week before concern got the best of me and I answered.

"Hello?"

"Stacey, how are you? I've been trying to call you! I really want to catch up!" she asked.

"I'm good," I answered slowly and carefully. "I've been liking my new college, and God's been doing amazing things in my life." For the next ten minutes or so, I shared with her how God had delivered me from homosexuality and how much I was transforming.

I stayed guarded the entire conversation. My heart was holding tightly to the freedom I'd spent an entire year obtaining, and I wanted no part of bondage anymore. I had learned about setting appropriate boundaries and with the grace of God, I was going to stick to them.

When I committed myself to the Lord, I also committed myself to praying for her wholeheartedly along with all my old friends who were still in the lifestyle. I wanted the opportunity to share Jesus with her. There was also a teensy part of me, however, that wanted to prove to her that I was really changed. During our conversation, she proceeded to ask how things were going with school and with me personally. I could tell she was skeptical about my claim to be "living for Christ." The fact that I wasn't pursuing women was very surprising to her, but I told her it was only by the power of Jesus that I was able to do this. She accepted it, but she ended the conversation by asking if we could meet up. After some initial hesitation, I agreed.

When I told my mom, I was meeting up with her, I thought she'd be excited that I was gonna be able to share Jesus with Danae. She wasn't. She felt like it was a trap from the enemy and to told me not to go. We completely disagreed, and even argued about it for the next few days, but I promised her I'd use wisdom.

Adrienne, one of my accountability partners from college, happened to come down to visit me at around this same time. I decided it would be a good idea for her to come with me to meet Danae, in an incognito sort of way. We planned for her to get to the meeting place ahead of me and Danae and sit at a table within view.

I woke up the day of the meeting nervous. It had been over a year since I'd seen Danae, and I wasn't really sure how I was gonna react. "Glorify Your name Lord, and guide me in this conversation," I remember saying as I got ready.

We pulled into the coffee shop. "Pray for me," I said to Adrienne. My hands were sweating, and I was shivering nervously. We walked in, choosing tables diagonal to each other. A few minutes later, Danae walked in.

Spotting me, she grinned and waved, quickly making her way over. I waved but deliberately stayed seated, not wanting to make any form of physical contact. I guess that surprised her, but she took a hint and just sat down. As we began to talk, I started having to constantly shut out the sexual memories that wanted to parade across my mind.

"So how's your mom?" she asked. We talked briefly about family and college, though I could tell she was using this as a precursor. We made some small talk for a while before she finally cut in. "So you said that God changed you? What do you mean by 'He changed you'?"

I was prepared. "You know, even though I was gay, I wasn't

happy," I began. "I think I had turned that way really as a cover up, to mask the hurt and rejection I was really dealing with."

"Yeah, but how is it different now?" she asked. "I mean, you were always a Christian, even when you were gay. Why do you have to stop being gay now? I mean, is it really that bad? What if you really love someone of the same sex?"

Again, I was prepared for this. I knew that she still wanted me, but despite old feelings creeping up, I wasn't going to let myself give in. So I started sharing my journey with God and what was happening in my new walk with Christ. I also shared some things that the Lord had put on my heart as I'd spent time in prayer for her and her family. I felt that there were specific things in her family that played a role in the sexual decisions she made. As I shared this with her, she was a little surprised at the fact that I knew those things and confirmed that they were true. This opened the door for me to really share the good news of the gospel with her, and how Jesus could absolutely set her free. In my heart, I really wanted to see her changed.

"Ok, so you said that God told you these things. But my question is this: if He knows these things, why didn't He do anything to stop them from happening to me?" she asked, her eyes filling with tears.

"Honestly, Danae, I don't know everything. I'm still learning," I said. "All I know is that the pleasure of the homosexual lifestyle doesn't even compare to the joy of the freedom I'm experiencing now. I still have to face temptation, but the power of God's Spirit strengthened me to overcome."

During this entire conversation, Adrienne was praying for me. We wrapped up our conversation and walked out to our cars. Before I got in the car, she grabbed my arm.

"Since we'll never see each other again, can we have sex one last time?"

All in one moment, I was as heavy as cement. *All of that Jesus talk and this was her response?*

"Come on Stacey, please," she pleaded. "This will be the last time ever. I miss you," she said, teary-eyed. My palms started perspiring again, as memories of previous sexual encounters flashed. For a brief moment, I felt the weakest I had ever felt in a long time, and I was scared I'd give in.

You're a new creation.

I could sense the gentle voice of the Holy Spirit inside of me reminding me of my newness in Christ, comforting me at the right time. "No Danae," I said firmly. "I'm sorry but I can't. It's not who I am anymore." Even with the Holy Spirit strengthening me, however, I could feel the pull to give in. "I'm about to head out. Danae, I agreed to meet up with you today, but this is the last time we ever need to see each other or talk again."

Tears started streaming down her face. I knew her hurt was genuine, but I also knew she believed wrongly. She thought I'd be able to fill a void in her heart that sexual abuse had created, and for a long time, I did. However, I knew she would never be able to find wholeness in another person. She'd only be able to find it in Christ.

I was shaky as I walked away, proud that I stood my ground but still sad that I had left her in such a state. I got in my car and drove away for a few minutes, and then went back to pick up Adrienne.

In my heart, I'd wanted her to be so moved by my own transformation that she would want what I had. But instead, I'd had to face the hardest temptation I'd faced in a year.

I still wasn't sure if meeting up with Danae was a good decision. However, I was truly filled with gratitude that God had proven that His Spirit in me was more powerful than any temptation I could possibly face. I knew I'd never see Danae again, but I committed myself to still pray for her. I hoped that one day, she would experience the same healing and love in Christ that I had.

Chapter 11

THE NEXT SCHOOL YEAR COULDN'T COME FAST ENOUGH.
I couldn't wait to see my friends and teammates and go to
prayer meetings again. I was also excited to get on the court
because I'd been working and training very hard and I was
ready to have a strong season.

I quickly settled into the familiar busyness of classes
and basketball training. "Ooooo girl, you lost weight!" my
teammates mused. I'd also become stronger, quicker, faster,
and obviously more skilled. The team could tell I was a
different player, and they even responded to me differently. I
began to connect with professors and built relationships with
them. *This is my year*, I thought.

As basketball season approached, our practice routine
started shifting. Our focus became more on plays, on which
players would start, and which players would be subs. In my

eyes, I was always in the top five talent-wise because of my hustle, my shot, and my quick eye.

One day at practice, my coach called out the starting lineup. "Gabby, Shaky, Mac, Brit, and Jo," he said. *This can't be right,* I thought. As he started moving people around, I ended up being one of the last players he chose. I was in disbelief. *There's no way this is right. Why am I being put with the bench players?* I was clearly a top player on my team. In fact, when I was still playing at my other college, we beat this very group of girls he was choosing for the top five.

Disappointment quickly dissolved into determination. *I'm gonna make him realize that I'm way better than this,* I thought. My strategy was to give his starters so much competition that it would be obvious he was making a mistake.

I worked my hardest, putting in effort over, above, and beyond what I'd ever done before. I did it not just that day, but for the next several weeks. My coach, however, didn't seem to notice, and kept grouping me with the lower caliber players. I constantly had to stave off discouragement, because it was obvious to me and everyone else on the team that I belonged in that top five.

During this particular time, I began reading the story of Moses. When Moses went to save his people, the Bible says that the Lord hardened the heart of Pharaoh. The fact that He did this had always seemed controversial to me. It almost seemed to me as if God was either deceiving Moses or working against Himself.

As I read the story this time, I couldn't help feeling like Moses. I felt like God had withdrawn His involvement in my life as far as basketball was concerned, and I couldn't understand how a coach could deny a player who was obviously at the top of the game.

Then, one day, it dawned on me: what if God was somehow *behind* the rejection of my coach to accomplish something different in my life? At first, this was just a thought, but I toyed with this idea for a while and made it a matter of prayer. This more this thought grew, the more it opened up to me like a light in a dark place, and I really felt a reassurance that this was exactly what was happening.

When season play started, I was prepared to handle what I expected would happen: I wouldn't get any playing time. God had prepared my heart for this through the story of Moses. I prayed before every practice and every game that God would help me keep my heart in the right place, knowing that I wouldn't get the opportunity to play.

While I never complained publicly, in private, I did complain and even cried. Even though I knew this would happen, I simply didn't understand why. Coaches from other colleges who had seen me play before would ask me why my coach never allowed me to play. It was always really tough answering that question, because I could always feel bitterness and resentment waiting for me to get offended. But I knew this was about more than basketball. I knew the hand of God was upon my life, and He wanted to do a work in me during this season.

I made it through basketball season with pain and tears, but I never allowed my lack of opportunity to deter my walk with God. So as the season closed, the competitive side of me wanted to prove to my coach that I could come back and be the best player on the team that next year. But first, because it was obvious that God was doing something in my life, I knew I needed to seek and ask Him first.

As I continued to pray, I started having a sense in my heart that the Lord was somehow leading me off the basketball team and into a better environment for spiritual growth. I continued to pray about this until there was no mistaking that this was the plan. *But no more basketball?* That was a tough pill for me to swallow. Basketball had been a part of me for so long, and playing college ball had always been my dream. But I'd had a taste of following God enough to know that the best and most fulfilling place I could be was in His will, so despite the sadness in my heart, I chose to trust where He was leading me.

I met with my coach and informed him that I wouldn't be returning to the team the next year. I left that meeting filled with hope and expectation, knowing that God was going to do something great in my life.

The very next day I received an email from one of the directors of the worship department. As I scanned it, I couldn't believe what I was reading: it was an invitation to travel with the worship band WITH a scholarship that exceeded what I was currently receiving for basketball!

I was stunned. It was so unreal. I had taken the step outside of my comfort zone and put my trust in God, and He had made my next step clear.

I knew this opportunity could have come from no one but Him. For one, the timing was too ridiculously on point for it to be just a coincidence. Secondly, only a few people in the entire campus knew I played drums, so the fact that I was now being offered a scholarship for it was nothing short of a divine miracle.

Chapter 12

MUSIC MINISTRY TRAVEL WAS SET TO BEGIN that summer, which meant lots of practices and prayer meetings for the next few months. The band was a totally different type of people than the basketball team, and at times, I felt a little out of my element. I had become accustomed to the relational dynamics on basketball teams, so I felt like I was constantly being pushed out of my comfort zone.

I struggled connecting with the music team. I would watch them interact during meetings, often wondering how they could be so open and so trusting with each other and wondering if and when I could ever get to that place. Instead of trying to build relationships with this new team, I found myself always retreating to spend quiet time with God. I loved spending time alone in prayer and studying the Bible, but after a while I started realizing that I was actually using it as an excuse to isolate myself from them. *But after all, why not?* I would think. If I spent all my time with God, I wouldn't have to deal with the awkward, hurtful, inconsistent, flaky, and rough parts of actually building relationships.

When we started leading worship for campus chapels and at other venues, I'd find myself withdrawing from everyone else during our breaks. For no reason at all, I would just get up and leave a hotel room or group setting to be alone. Even though it was lonely, at least I was safe. It was so much easier than having to guess where a friendship could possibly go. And when we were together as group, I could only be around the band for a certain amount of time before I started feeling uncomfortable. They probably thought I was weird, but it didn't concern me.

As we continued to travel, it became crystal clear to me that I still dealt heavily with rejection. It probably looked to them like I disliked them or was just awkward. Their attempts to build a friendship with me made me see that I was continuously hindered by the fear of people rejecting me. I didn't understand why I always expected the worst and protected myself from others by withdrawing. I knew I had enough personality to hold a deep and even meaningful conversation, but I never expected or pursued anything beyond that. Rejection had become so deeply rooted in who I was that it was like an undetected undercurrent, influencing all my relational decisions.

I normalized my condition for as long as I could, not

making concentrated efforts at friendships and being okay with it. I could tell there was an invisible wall between me and the rest of the music team, but nobody ever addressed it and I certainly wasn't going to.

As the weeks turned into months and we kept traveling, my tendency to withdraw started to bother me, and I began to desire to pursue real friendships. I didn't want to live as a product of my past, so I decided to try to step out and make myself friendly to the rest of the team.

To my surprise, it was easier than I thought. I started sparking conversations with people, listening to their stories, and allowing them to become vulnerable with me. I discovered that it was easy for me to tell my story too, because I'd become accustomed to giving my testimony about God changing my life around and I loved talking about Him. I still couldn't bring myself to have consistent, every day conversations, so I had yet to develop any real friendships.

As I continued letting down my guard and intentionally making conversations, I started to get past some of the awkward humps that had stopped me before. But as I got more comfortable conversing with people and relationships started to form, I began to notice that I was always the listener, and when it came time for me to talk or share something from my heart, they'd either cut me off or change the subject. It went that way with almost everyone, so after a while, I started closing myself in.

Through a series of events, I became the assistant leader of campus prayer. As I led prayer meetings, I began to notice a girl named Jenna who always seemed to be friendly and caring. Unknowingly yet purposely, I would watch her interact with others. I'd see her nod, as she listened, to someone's story. I noticed her reassuring pats on people's shoulders, her hugs, and her tears. *Hmm,* I thought. *This looks like the kind of Christian female friendship I want to have.*

Over the next few weeks, I intentionally sought out opportunities to have conversations with her. We'd laugh, joke, and share our passion about God with each other until we were late for class. I would always leave our conversations feeling light-hearted and encouraged. I began to be more and more excited and hopeful that I could actually be building a real, healthy female friendship for the first time in my life.

At first, we would just see each other at prayer meetings. I was still a bit apprehensive about overinvesting myself, but her warm and friendly demeanor invited me to trust and open myself up to her, so little by little, I did just that.

Even though Jenna was the type of friend I wanted, I still proceeded forward with much caution and fear. I didn't want this friendship to end up as shallow as all the others had.

But with every conversation, my heart became more and more reassured. It was obvious that Jenna didn't just want help or prayer. She genuinely wanted a friendship, and she was as invested in building one as much as I was.

We started hanging out outside of school, and I would often go to her family's house. Several months into the friendship, her family started going through a difficult time. By this time, she and I had become very close friends, and I was there for her to help her walk through this season. I prayed for her and her family non-stop, and God began to give me dreams about what they were dealing with and the wisdom on how to handle situations.

I would share these things with her, and she'd be shocked at the level of detail I knew. As I continued to share solutions I felt the Lord was giving me, her family started implementing what I was suggesting, and they began to see improvement.

I was so invested in her life, spent so much time in prayer for her, and had so much insight and wisdom for her that our relationship began to develop a client/counselor dynamic. Over the next few weeks and months, every time we'd hang out, I ended up counseling her through some issue she was dealing with. That eventually morphed into a dependent and codependent relationship where she was overly dependent on me, and I became dependent on her depending on me.

I had to put a stop to this.

"Jenna, this relationship is unhealthy," I finally told her one day. "I think we need to draw some healthy boundaries and take a break from each other for a while."

She looked hurt and stared at me silently for a moment. "Okaaaay," she finally said. She did a good job of masking her offense, but I could still feel it. We decided that we would no longer hangout, text, or talk on the phone.

Despite the fact that I needed this break, I felt like I had failed. I had opened my heart, shared myself, and made myself very vulnerable to another female in a platonic way for the first time in my life. This wasn't the end I had been hoping for.

I stayed discouraged for a while. I thought I was finally at the point where I would be able to have relationships that weren't shallow. I felt like it was my fault that the relationship ended up unhealthy, and I wanted to continue to seek God for healing and deliverance.

A year later the prayer organization moved me from being the assistant to being the leader. I felt unqualified and unprepared, but I was committed to seeing God move. Knowing I still dealt with rejection and needed healing, I tried to be as intentional as possible about how I was leading the team. I didn't want to lead from a place of frustration, despite the unresolved issues in my soul.

During prayer meetings, I saw God perform miracles, signs and wonders on a weekly basis. Professors, students, and families were saved, parents were healed of cancer, and athletes were healed from injuries, among many other miracles.

Despite all the amazing manifestations of the love of God I was seeing, however, I still felt very alone. I battled daily with thoughts of quitting, and rejection still followed me around everywhere.

I prayed that no one would be able to tell.

Chapter 13

IN THE SPRING OF 2011, I graduated and was getting ready to transition into the graduate program. I knew it was time for me to pass on the responsibility of leading campus prayer to someone else and take time to focus more on myself. My schedule eased into a flow of working and taking classes, but I still wanted to be present at prayer meetings.

At one meeting, I noticed a young lady praying passionately on the microphone. I studied her, ignited in my spirit by the intensity and obvious passion of her prayer. *Who is that?* I thought. I continued to watch her throughout the meeting and could tell that she was genuine about seeking God. I had to meet her.

"Hey, I'm Stacey," I said after the meeting was over. "I noticed you praying up there and I don't think I've ever seen you here. Where are you from?"

"I'm Sophia, and this is my first time here," she said, smiling. We continued to converse, and I couldn't help but be drawn to the way she passionately talked about God and how serious she seemed about her walk with Him.

In my heart, I was still interested in finding and building a healthy female friendship. Caution in my soul still counseled me to be guarded, but I longed for the kind of companionship and fellowship I had with Jenna again.

We began to fellowship more and more, and our friendship began to grow. I started to realize that I wasn't the only one doing the investing. Out of the overflow of her relationship with God, she also encouraged me. We would talk for hours and started hanging out on a consistent basis. We'd constantly share our experiences with God with one another, and this new friendship started genuinely becoming an iron-sharpening-iron type of relationship. Once again, I started building excitement because I had craved this for so long.

As the months went by, we challenged one another to the point of disagreements and frustrating moments of self-reflection. These things only served to further our growth in God and helped us mature in Him, strengthening our relationship even further.

After a few months, my life almost revolved around Sophia. We hung out after class, during lunch, and on weekends. We went to events together and spent the night in each other's rooms. She didn't need a counseling session every day, and I loved that.

And without realizing it, I became too attached.

She was a spiritually healthy person, and I clung to her like a lifeline. I was always thinking about what she was doing, when we'd hang out next, and I was *always* praying for her. I was determined not to lose this friendship. After all, where would I ever again find such a good friend?

The little, rejected Stacey inside of me was experiencing what I'd always desired: a godly, healthy and pure relationship with another female.

I noticed myself starting to become increasingly obsessed with her opinions and feelings. I cared about them more than anyone else's, including God's. When she was sad I was sad, when she was mad I was mad, and when she was happy I was happy. It was almost like I was one with her.

And before long, the dynamics in this relationship also began to shift. As she began to go through difficult seasons in her life and I walked her through them in prayer, I found myself being more of a counselor than actually having a friend. She started depending on me too much, and I began to depend on her depending on me. It was starting to look like a repeat of my friendship with Jenna.

Somewhere in the midst of everything, we had transitioned from being mutually encouraging to being consistently toxic. As an outsider, you would have thought we were actually dating, and in a sense, that's what it was like. I almost felt like I was back in a relationship with an old girlfriend as a homosexual. I was consumed with her opinions, and she was depending on me instead of God.

When it got to this point, I knew it was time for me to completely cut the relationship off. This was now my second time doing this. What was I doing wrong?

"Sophia, our relationship has become way too unhealthy. We need to take a break from each other," I told her one day.

She agreed, which made things easier, although I knew from my first experience that the process of separation would be challenging. Almost overnight, we agreed to cut off all communication, all hanging out, and pretty much seeing each other altogether.

It was a difficult decision, but a necessary one. It also made me reflect a lot on why this seemed to be the trend. What else did I need to do to get fully delivered? What else did I need to do to finally be able to have healthy relationships?

Chapter 14

I KNEW I NEEDED HELP BEYOND what I'd been able to obtain on my own thus far, and I deeply craved the fullness of complete freedom. By this point, God had changed me so much that I no longer had any sexual desire for women, which I was thankful for. However, my experience with Jenna and Sophia showed me I still struggled building healthy female friendships.

I wanted to be completely free from any and all rejection. I found out that a friend of mine had a mom who was currently in a ministry that focused on healing and deliverance. When I learned that, I knew I just had to meet with her. "Please please PLEASE call her and set up an appointment for me!" I told him, practically begging.

She agreed to come to the campus and do a deliverance session with me. I could hardly contain my excitement, and when I shared with a few friends what was going to happen, they wanted to be in on it too.

At the session, there were about seven of us there. After praying, she began. "What you've walked through in your past affects you on all levels," she said. "It affects you not just physically, but psychologically, spiritually, and emotionally as well." She went on to explain that just as medical conditions can be passed down, so also can issues in any of these four realms.

"If something traumatizing happened in your life, there are emotional wounds that open, which calls for inner healing and deliverance."

As I listened, flashbacks paraded my mind like movie clips. I remembered my grandma's house and my uncle touching me. I saw myself as a young child, all alone with too much to handle. I thought about my dad not being there when I needed him, and not being able, for years, to talk candidly with my mom about my struggles.

"We're going to start the deliverance process," she said. "The first thing I want you to do is ask God to forgive you and anyone in your family who has opened the door to anything contrary to the word of God." We then asked God to cleanse us of the habits, addictions, perversion, sicknesses and diseases these open doors had brought.

A few of my friends began to shake, throw up and cry. The minister noticed that I was just praying and worshiping the Lord, so she asked me to assist her as she prayed for them.

After two hours passed, many of my friends were getting set free, but I still hadn't been prayed for. *Maybe I shouldn't have invited them,* I thought. *I'm the one who really wanted this in the first place!*

I could tell the minister was starting to wrap up. I tried my best not to get upset, and I asked if she could at least pray over me before she left. "Sure, hun," she said. "What do you want prayer for?" I quickly began to tell her my life story, focusing on the homosexuality, perversion, abuse, and molestation. She began to pray for me, and I felt the presence of God. However, nothing dramatic happened. I didn't shake, scream, or throw up, so I wasn't really sure if I was free. *Maybe I didn't ask the right thing,* I thought. I left the meeting a little discouraged, but thankful for the insight I'd gained. I knew I needed to keep pursuing restoration for myself.

As I got busier with ministry, however, I found that I was constantly putting this pursuit on the backburner. I would wake up very early, before anyone else on the ministry team, and pray to make sure my personal issues weren't going to interfere with either the team or the ministry. *I wonder if I'll ever be completely delivered,* I would often think.

I reached a point where I was too overwhelmed with the cry of my own soul for freedom and decided to step back completely from ministry to pursue full healing.

For the next couple years, I spent all of my time worshiping, praying, reading the Word, and finishing graduate school. I had become so consumed with why I wasn't healed that I ended up depressed.

I found a ministry in Philadelphia, Pennsylvania that ministered healing and deliverance over the phone. I made an appointment, and within a week I received a phone call from the ministry to begin a deliverance session.

The woman who was walking me through deliverance started praying for me and identified some things that had me bound through the years like lust, homosexuality, anger and fear. "I command these spirits to leave by the power of Jesus Christ," she said.

By the time the session was over, I felt like some things had lifted off of me. I was encouraged because I felt some freedom; however, I didn't feel like I was completely and fully free. Over the course of the next few weeks, I faithfully kept my heart before God. There were times that I was just overwhelmed at how badly I wanted complete healing. I was also frustrated because I didn't want to continue depending on people for the healing that God had promised me. I was determined to have it, so I began to fast, pray, and research all I could to get better understanding.

During this time, I was sitting under a ministry I felt I could learn from. I had spent months attending every service, absorbing every teaching, and even playing drums for them. One day, a few of the leaders confronted me about a situation. They shared that the community perceived me a certain way, a negative way, and I was hurt. I felt completely rejected and left out. As a result, I became angry, very short, very distant, and very inwardly focused.

The pain I was looking to get healed of actually intensified at this time, and I was so overwhelmed that I didn't want to live anymore. No one, it seemed, understood me, and at this point, I wasn't sure if anyone ever would.

One day after a service, I met a woman and immediately was drawn to her. I could feel the power of healing over her as soon as we started talking. She mentioned that she had a ministry for healing and deliverance, and I got excited. *Maybe this is who I've been waiting for.* It seemed to be perfect timing. "Would you be willing to walk me through some inner healing and deliverance?" I asked.

"Of course," she answered warmly, putting me even more at ease. Maybe, just maybe, this would bring about my full deliverance.

The day of the session, I felt so much peace, and I walked in with great expectation. She started by explaining the love of the Father to me like I'd never heard it before. She asked the Holy Spirit to fill the room and to lead us through healing. "Holy Spirit you are the great Healer, so we welcome you in this meeting to reveal and heal the places in our lives that need restoration and purification," she said to start the meeting.

During the session, we re-visited many events and places of trauma in my life, such as being unwanted, being molested and abused, being called a tomboy, and many other things. Her tenderness made it easier to explore and press in to the painful events of my past.

As we worked through these events one by one, the main issue that surfaced from everything was rejection. As I began to visually and mentally experience those moments in my life again. All of a sudden, I saw a man standing before me. I knew it was the Lord. "I was there the whole time," He said.

When He said that, every wall in me collapsed. I had always felt like I was never protected and that no one was there for me. Hearing Him say that was like the answer to my heart's deepest question for decades. After the session, I felt so free, and it was a feeling I'd never felt before. When I finally got in my car to drive home, I cried for an hour straight. His love was so powerful that it exposed deception, feelings of rejection, insecurities, and every evil thing that the enemy had planted in my heart over the years. I felt pure, I felt whole, and I felt renewed. I knew that I had truly encountered the REAL God.

I took that encounter and began to build and develop from it. I continued to go for more sessions and did check-ups with her every now and then.

After that experience, my life took a major turn in a positive direction. To this day, I've been able to walk through self-deliverance and gain freedom in many other areas of my life. I've learned that despite what I've suffered, I don't have to walk as a victim of what other people have or haven't done to me. At the end of the day, what matters most, what has helped me come out and stay out, is this:

My Father loves me, accepts me, and never leaves me to handle life on my own.

PART III:
HELPING YOU GET FREE

FROM MY LIFESTYLE AS A LESBIAN, I learned that there are both demons that need to be cast out and wounds that need to be healed for a person to walk in complete restoration. People who need healing and deliverance will be able to function in everyday life but will always have limitations and areas where they will keep seeing cycles of bondage.

Deliverance refers to the removing of demons or demonic influence over a person's life. Demons are evil spirits sent to kill, steal, and destroy the things that God has planned for you. God has a kingdom and purpose for your life, but Satan also has a kingdom and purpose for your life. It's up to you to decide which kingdom he or she will allow to influence your life.

Demons can gain influence in our lives through open doors and through generational curses. A person can open the door to demons through activities such as palm reading, witchcraft, sexual immorality and other things contrary to the standards of God's word. For example, my mother opened the door to lust and perversion when she engaged in sexual immorality with my father during college. This choice opened the door for demons to influence my life with lust, promiscuity, and a lifestyle full of things rooted in lust. Without deliverance in these areas, I would have found myself in bondage to an unbreakable hold of perversion.

Generational curses are also a way demons can enter our lives. Generational curses are sins that are passed down from one generation to the next. Sin, just like sicknesses and diseases have the ability to transfer from one generation to the next. All four of my grandparents dealt with sexual abuse, sexual immorality and rejection. These very same struggles were passed to me, even though I didn't want them and would never have chosen them.

Thankfully, I was able to both break free and stop these curses from being passed down to my children through deliverance and healing.

Healing takes place when an individual's emotional and psychological self returns to the healthy, normal state God intended. Events in our lives, from the time we're conceived, have an imperative impact on the way we think and feel. I was wounded from being taken advantage of sexually, being rejected by my parents, being talked about by church members, and feeling alone. These events caused broken areas in my thought processes and emotions. I needed emotional and psychological restoration, because these fractured areas started to shape my personality. I began to take the nature of a quiet, timid and distant individual to the point that I thought that was just who I was.

This wasn't the truth, however. What I really needed was healing in the wounded and fractured places of my soul-my mind, will and emotions. In my story, I talked about how I sought out people for personal ministry. It was in these moments that God began to heal the incomplete parts of me. Seeking out this kind of help was essential, and I believe if I hadn't received full healing, I would have eventually fallen back into the lifestyle of homosexuality.

Now, throughout my healing process, I still faced moments of temptation. This is because our flesh desires the things of this world and not godly things. Many people have asked questions like "how have you not gone back?", "are you ever tempted?", or "what if you feel like you are born that way?" My answer to this is simply that if there is enough power to save me, there is enough power to keep me.

Genesis 3 sets the stage for explaining why human beings struggle to begin with. Adam and Eve ate the fruit of the tree of the knowledge of good and evil, and it became the moment that human beings were capable of sinning. Their disobedience opened up the entire human race to evils such as murder, rape, addictions, abuse, lust, anger, and even homosexuality. So if you ask questions like *can an individual be tempted by homosexuality?* or *can an individual be born into sin or homosexuality?* the answer is yes. Psalm 51:5 says, "True, I was born guilty, I was a sinner from the moment my mother conceived me".

It's possible to be born in sin and even into homosexuality. In fact, this is precisely why God sent His Son to die for us and our sins. If we didn't have sin in our lives, we would never need Jesus. We need God to be able to live for God. We can be born into sin, but we can also be delivered by the power of God.

A story that gives a great example of how God can deliver and bring individuals out of bondage and into freedom is the story of the Israelites. This group of people was in bondage for many years. However, they became discontent with slavery and cried out because they were tired of being slaves. God heard their cry and sent a man by the name of Moses to deliver them out of their bondage. The Israelites were set free, but it took a process to get them from where they were to where they needed to be.

Likewise, it took a process for me to come out of bondage. After walking through healing and deliverance, I still had to maintain my freedom and walk with Christ. If a sick person goes to the doctor, the doctor will give that individual medication and instructions on how to get healed. However, it's up to that person to maintain the responsibility given to them by the doctor.

I had to apply this same concept concerning my lifestyle and maintaining freedom. After giving back my life to the Lord, I knew I would face challenges and uncertainties, but I knew that I would need to persevere if I wanted to see the freedom I was after. To help facilitate my freedom, there are three practices I implemented that I found to be effective that can also be utilized by anyone who is seeking deliverance in any way. You need to understand your identity, have accountability, and set solid boundaries.

IDENTITY

No matter who you are and what you need freedom from, you need to have a proper understanding of your identity. Identity refers to who you are and how you perceive yourself to be. It encompasses the quality and beliefs people hold within themselves and the way they express it to the people around them. A person's behavior and outlook on life is directly influenced by his or her identity and concept of him or herself. However, the only way to know who you are is to know the One who created you. Without a greater understanding of the Creator, one can never fully understand creation.

Growing up, all I knew was what I saw, which was abuse, perversion, rejection and working hard to make it in life. My view of myself was shaped by this, and I saw myself as a survivor, a hard worker, an introvert, and a lustful person. On my journey toward freedom, I began to abandon all that I had cultivated about myself and pursued God, through reading the Bible, spending time in prayer and worship, and surrounding myself with people who loved Jesus. I began to discover who God was, His character, His desires, His history, His purpose, His plans, His love, His likes, His dislikes, and His language.

My identity not only as a woman began to be restored, but my identity as a daughter began to develop as well.

I didn't realize it, but my mentality for so long had been that of a slave. I was bound and I always felt like I had to work my way into a right standing with Christ. However, I came to realize that the overwhelming love of my Father never changed regardless if I was good, bad, holy, dressed as a woman or dressed as a man. Once I began to gain a better understanding of my Heavenly Father, my whole perspective changed.

To do life without a proper understanding of your identity is to do life as an orphan. Orphans and slaves live and look at life completely differently than sons, daughters and individuals who know their true identity. My parents never planned to have me, and I was just product of their irresponsibility. I lived as an orphan because I thought I was an accident to my earthly parents, but I received freedom from understanding how my Heavenly Father saw me.

A son or a daughter obtains his or her identity from where he or she originated. Geographically speaking, a person cannot get to a destination without knowing where they're currently located. In terms of identity, to be able to know where you're located is to know where you came from. In other words, a son or a daughter can only know who they are when they know where and who they come from. You find your *origin* when you find God. You find your *why* when you find God. You find your *who* when you find God. And in the midst of it all, you learn that you don't need to exert unnecessary energy trying to prove yourself.

Knowing your identity is so vital that even God thought it important to make a public announcement of Jesus as his "Son". In the New Testament, Scripture tells us that the heavens were opened and the Father declared over Jesus, saying, "This is my Son whom I am well pleased". God the Father made it a point to declare sonship over Jesus before Jesus experienced temptation and before His ministry fully started. This is very important because how he responded to every temptation from that point on was from a position of understanding who the Father said He was.

We fall or give in to temptation as a result of what we think we need. Adam and Eve yielded to temptation because they thought they were gaining something that they actually already had. Knowing your identity will determine what you will or will not be subject to and will be displayed in the way you live your life.

Proverbs 23:7 expresses the idea that whatever a person thinks within himself, he will become. Our thoughts play a part in how we feel, which then affects the way we behave and express ourselves. So identity is rooted in the way a person psychologically, emotionally and physiologically perceives himself.

BOUNDARIES

Another practice I implemented as I matured in Christ was to set boundaries. I knew that the things I allowed around me determined my healing, deliverance and growth. God Himself gave limitations and boundaries to Adam and Eve in the Garden of Eden in order for them to remain blessed and sustain what was given to them. He allowed them to eat the fruit of any tree except for one, which He warned them would bring consequences if they even touched it.

Another great example of boundaries in the Bible is when God sent Moses to deliver the Israelites from the bondage of Pharaoh and the system of Egypt. When the Israelites were set free and they entered into a new place, God gave boundaries and instructions not to go into specific cities. God commanded them not to mingle with other men, women and children, and in doing so, He was limiting who He wanted them to fellowship and worship with. God obviously knows that who an individual is connected to has the ability to influence what the individual does, says and believes.

The Israelites disobeyed God's commands, and as a result, they found themselves worshipping other gods, complaining, and in dangerous circumstances. However, when the Israelites obeyed God's instructions, they were also blessed beyond measure and impacted the nations around them. There are blessings both in obedience to God and in the boundaries He gives us.

God's instruction comes through His written Word, but it is up to us to implement and execute these guidelines. When God created Adam and Eve, He gave them a set of instructions that consisted of boundaries, but it was up to them to take responsibility. Boundaries foster an environment for growth, but when they are crossed, confusion is conceived and leads to destruction.

Just imagine what would happen if there were no boundaries on the freeway and in the streets around your home. There would be wrecks, confusion, destruction, robberies and deaths galore. Boundaries help protect and guard our lives from danger and chaos.

In my personal life, I set specific boundaries around myself in order to heal and grow. A number of things I did to establish my boundaries consisted of removing things that were connected to my past and throwing out anything that was contrary to God's Word. This included phone numbers, music, clothes, gifts, social media and any other things that the Lord asked of me. I also took some time away from social media and gave myself to God in extensive fasting and prayer. I limited what I watched on television as well as certain movies at the movie theater.

I was particular about the kinds of conversations I allowed myself to engage in during my time of healing as well. I tried to keep these conversations edifying, Christ centered, and safe for vulnerable issues in my life. Some people felt like I lived my life in a bubble, but I knew boundaries had to be kept in place. Think about it this way: if a medical patient received surgery, that individual would be required to follow instructions from their doctor that would give limitations on what the person could and could not do. The same idea applies to limitations in our lives as we pursue wholeness.

I've found that boundaries set me up for productivity, purpose, and blessings. Without them, I would be far from my potential and the things that God had ordained for me. People who want to stay healthy, become millionaires, gain a superb education, and be successful in life all have a set of things that they can and cannot do. These individuals must have boundary lines they will not cross or allow anyone else to cross in order to maintain and develop their goals. It should also be this way for those who profess to be part of the family of God. In John 5:19, the Bible says that Jesus only did what He saw His Father doing.

Before time, God ordained blessings within the boundary lines of marriage between a man and a woman that other relationships will never experience. What I've come to understand is that there is always a measure of pleasure outside of God's boundaries, but the fullness of God's blessing, joy, prosperity, and purpose can only be found in God. It's not cliche, because the one who created everything knows the extent and potential of His creation.

Creation can never tell its creator the best option for something because creation's level of understanding is limited to its experiences. If God instituted and created something to be established in His eternal wisdom and understanding, we have to understand that there is a treasure in it. Even for those who have genuine same-sex attractions, we have to understand that there are thousands of people all over the world who have desires for things outside of what God has already established as good. The sin that Adam and Eve committed in the book of Genesis opened the door to evil desires, and from then on in the Word of God, you can read about individuals who desired and did things contrary to God's order. That's why we need deliverance, healing, and the power of the Holy Spirit to live in a world of systems opposite of God's. When we set boundaries in our lives, we make room for God to come in and establish His desires and ways within us so that we're restored back to the original way He planned for us to be.

ACCOUNTABILITY

Another practice I implemented in my life to remain whole in Christ is accountability. The concept of accountability pertains to taking responsibility for certain standards and abiding by a set level of expectations. Accountability can seem very challenging because you are in a very vulnerable place and it requires you to be very honest with other people.

I was a person who always lived in my head and processed things within myself. However, when it came to being accountable I had to be okay with making myself vulnerable to someone in order to get the results I desired. I started opening up and being accountable little by little. I opened up and shared my testimony with a group of friends that I trusted and asked for them to check on me and keep me in their prayers. I knew if these people prayed for me, the Holy Spirit would reveal things to them about me that would demand maturity and spiritual growth. Over the years, these same people would correct me and I was open to receiving from them because they had kept me accountable out of love and wanted God's BEST for my life.

For me, accountability consisted of weekly checkups, monthly checkups, or random pop-ins whenever I was struggling. Accountability requires you to take responsibility for your actions as well as gives you confidence because you're not doing life by yourself. One of the worst places to be when you're going through something in your life is in isolation. Isolation is the garden for dysfunction and destruction. It's always good to have a second pair of eyes, another opinion, an open heart, and listening ears of another person, even if you disagree with what they suggest to you. Having another perspective can provide you with another way of seeing a situation in a way you may not have thought of before. Healthy accountability allows you to ask hard questions without being judged.

Once, I remember having a meeting with a mentor for an accountability session. When I shared with her what I was struggling with, she made it clear that my struggles and challenges were a part of my flesh, but that my Abba Father wasn't intimidated by my weakness.

Her response brought a lot of healing to me for two reasons. One, she put my challenge in perspective. She helped me see it in a way that made it look smaller and more conquerable. Secondly, her view of me didn't change and she saw God's hand on my life.

Accountability can be a very powerful tool that can transform an individual's life forever. Honesty and consistency are two important components in the healing process and have potential to make or break your process. When a person has the opportunity to be honest without being judged, he or she is far less likely to feel shame. Without shame, truth can fully be expressed. Once the truth is expressed and a person can let out the things that are weighing them down, it brings them a sense of liberty.

However, in order for full freedom to take place, being honest cannot be a one-time thing-it must happen on a consistent basis. Consistency builds strength, and strength builds confidence.

CONCLUSION

The world has always used the phrase "coming out" to describe an individual finally expressing who he or she really is as a homosexual, transgender, or the like. However, the heart behind how I came out and stayed out of bondage was to testify of the power of God. The love of God brought me out of a lifestyle and kept me out of that lifestyle, and He can do the same for you.

"With men, this is impossible, but with God, all things are possible."
- *Matthew 19:26 (NKJV)*

About The Author

Astacia Jones is the founder of Life Abandon Ministries, an organization that employs counseling, teaching, and training to empower people to walk in their God-given purpose. She has a heart to serve the next generation and believes this happen through the impartation of the knowledge of God.

A native of Houston, Texas, Astacia currently resides in the DFW metroplex. She holds a Bachelor's degree in Counseling and a Master's degree in Clinical Counseling and Psychology. She has served both youth and young adults as a high school behavioral counselor, a basketball coach, and a mentor.

Astacia travels the country telling her testimony of how the power of God saved her life in 2008. Through Life Abandon Ministries, she also hosts yearly youth conferences that focus on helping youth and young adults identify their purpose and undergo training to become leaders. Through these conferences, she's been able to see hundreds of youth encounter the heart of God.

Made in the USA
Coppell, TX
14 January 2022

71636194R00073